THE LOST ART OF TRAVEL

THE LOST ART OF TRAVEL

A Handbook for the Modern Adventurer

VIC DARKWOOD

JOHN MURRAY

First published in 2006 by John Murray (Publishers)
A division of Hodder Headline

A CIP catalogue record for this title is available from the British Library

ISBN-13 978-0-7195-6065-1
ISBN-10 0-7195-6065-9

Typeset in Walbaum Book 9.25/13pt by
Servis Filmsetting Ltd, Manchester

Printed and bound by Clays Ltd, St Ives plc

Hodder Headline policy is to use papers that are natural, renewable and recyclable products and made from wood grown in sustainable forests. The logging and manufacturing processes are expected to conform to the environmental regulations of the country of origin.

John Murray (Publishers)
338 Euston Road
London NW1 3BH

CONTENTS

INTRODUCTION

It is widely acknowledged that a man who develops a taste for travel in his youth sows the seeds of an enthusiasm that will last a lifetime. An acquaintance of mine, a military man, once confided to me, over an Armagnac or two, that during twelve years of marriage, his wife had gradually come to remind him of a bay mare packhorse that he had hired when exploring the interior of Asia Minor. There was something about the colour of her hair, her large trusting eyes, her fondness for sugar and the timbre of her laugh that slowly began to insinuate the similarity. He asked me if I found this disturbing, and I replied 'Not at all, dear fellow.' It was quite plain to me that my friend was pining for the cut and thrust of adventure and aching to travel once more. If it were not for his family responsibilities, I have absolutely no doubt he would be off like a shot.

So, whilst he is young, firm of limb, and free from the afflictions of parenthood and gout, every man should consider spending time exploring the world. After all, there are few occupations more hearty, broadening and educational for a youngster than to engage in travel; be it a fully-fledged expedition to Jacareacanga, a cultural tour of Umbria or a soggy day trip to Hartlepool. Science tells us that a three-month jaunt into an uncharted interior will expand the temporal lobes more fully than three years reading 'tourism studies' at one of our lesser universities, and that a youngster in his late twenties with a few solid years of travel under his belt is ⁹⁄₁₆ths more likely to become a leader of men than his sedentary counterpart. As Francis Galton puts it in his invaluable *The Art of Travel* in 1872:

> If you have health, a great craving for adventure, at least a moderate fortune, and can set your heart on a definite objective, which old travellers do not think impracticable, then travel by all means. I believe that no career, in time of peace, can offer to you more advantages than that of a traveller.

The advantages of travel are incontestable. Every young man of vim dreams of heading out into the world in the hope of making a name for himself, getting into all sorts of scrapes and returning home several years later to publish his hair-raising memoirs. His appetite will no doubt have been whetted by reading such volumes as *Tom Cringle's Log* (1833), *An Englishman in a Harem* (1887), and *Alone with the Hairy Ainu* (1893). But fame and fortune are not the only benefits of travel:

Travelling is a recreation to be recommended, especially to those whose

The Hairy Ainu – just one of the remarkable spectacles that can inspire the inquisitive man to travel

employment is sedentary, who are engaged in abstract studies, whose minds have been sunk in a state of morbid melancholy by hypochondriasis; or, by what is worst of all, who have a lack of domestic felicity.

The Traveller's Oracle, Dr William Kitchiner, 1827

Yes indeed, travel is one of the best techniques of improving one's general well-being and avoiding the iniquities of a less than perfect married life.

Traditionally a man lacking 'domestic felicity' will spend most of his waking hours at the club, loitering in his library or planting up geraniums in the greenhouse, and in this respect travel can be regarded as a highly effective trans-migratory potting shed that keeps a fellow out of harm's way, and consequently his marriage healthier than it has any real right to be.

In my own travels I am invariably accompanied by my wife, Mrs Darkwood, and we strictly adhere to the rule of travelling in the *grand style vieux Anglais*, eschewing the modern-day vulgarities of package tour and tourist outing in favour of letting ourselves be guided by the classic handbooks of yesteryear.

There was a time when an Englishman was welcomed everywhere abroad, providing the natives with useful gift items such as beads, mirrors and brightly-coloured ribbons, relieving them of the burden of developing their mineral deposits and asking nothing in return. But sadly, to my mind, there is a worrying trend amongst today's callow wayfarers. Now, instead of following the great British tradition of journeying the globe taking measurements, civilizing nations and climbing to the top of anything that looks daunting enough, today's youth seem to regard the planet as if it were their own personal amusement park.

The antics of today's juvenile travellers can be distressing. Partying till dawn, swimming with dolphins, filling their hair with baubles and knots, marking their flesh with needles and transporting their chattels in large dorsal sacks seems to be the order of the day. It should be obvious to anyone that strapping items of luggage to one's back, like a common Sherpa, can do great damage to the line of a finely cut linen jacket; but I gather this is of little consequence to so-called 'backpackers' who clad themselves in gaily-hued polyester, replete with new-fangled zip fasteners, Velcro and 'popper' buttons.

On the other side of the coin, the older traveller is rarely seen to be much better. Charabanc parties hell-bent on taking in the sights and fearful of bowel complaints will slavishly stick to a rigid itinerary, eschewing anywhere off the beaten track and shunning contact with the indigenous peoples and local food. As the *Tourists' Annual* notes as early as 1867 (and very little has changed):

> The rapid style of 'doing' the Continent is simply intolerable. There is no relaxation, no recreation or pleasure whatever in hurrying through things like a steam engine. Five-eighths of the British and American tourists abroad look as peevish and discontented as if they were doing penance instead of seeking for pleasure. They grumble at this and grumble at that, express here and express there, two castles and a cathedral before dinner, a picture-gallery after that, and then the opera, and off by five o'clock the next morning; that is the general style of the Tourist Vorax abroad.

It is quite plain that the majority of today's travellers are still not doing it right. Blundering off on a jaunt ill-prepared and blithely pooh-poohing the lessons of precedent, a young buck is setting himself up for a fall. In all likelihood he will eventually find himself in a merry pickle, locked up in the slammer or attempting to survive solely on a diet of twigs. Older voyagers, with their luncheon boxes and tick lists, might just as profitably stay at home, and spend their final years playing bingo or watching travel programmes on their television sets. Maybe it is time for contemporary voyagers, young and old, male and female, rich and poor, to seek the advice and wisdom of a previous generation.

A brief glance around the travel section of today's bookshops will convince the reader that there is a paucity of literature dealing with the true nitty-gritty of the traveller's art. Legion are the volumes dedicated to remote regions of the globe, to charts and maps, to family 'activity' holidays and to tourist guides for popular destinations; but, quite inexplicably, precious few seem willing to broach essential topics such as the avoidance of vermin, the practical theory of tea-making, catching ducks by hand, using ant hills as ovens, or digging a well with a pointy stick.

Travel writers from 1800 to the 1920s exhibited no such reticence, cataloguing all aspects of travel with an eye for detail that would give a sparrowhawk a run for its money. In guides ranging from accounts of early nineteenth-century expeditions to the first publications of John Murray and Baedeker; from treatises on the arts of cycling and ballooning to the singular musings of Frank Tatchell, Vicar of Midhurst, nothing is left to chance, no area of interest to the traveller uncharted, and no source of danger or difficulty neglected.

A reading public, surely bored rigid by today's anodyne travel books, is deserving of a new and wide-ranging compendium of these

classic writers. Within these pages I have selected a broad range of travel advice gleaned from genuine publications, and I have designed it to be of interest not only to the conventional tourist visiting the great cities of the world and the youngster hell-bent on 'having a good time' as he marauds about the globe, but also to those of a more serious and expeditionary bent determined to 'rough it' far from the comforts of civilization. Along the way there will be plenty of time to investigate the correct way to prepare for various modes of transport, some interesting facts about the countries you are likely to visit, and plenty of 'local colour'.

I sincerely hope that the following extracts instil in you a wanderlust to be satiated only by prising yourself from your armchair, gathering up your portmanteau and umbrella, donning your favourite tweed hunting jacket and setting off on a sterling voyage of discovery.

CHAPTER THE FIRST

Concerning the Selection of

SUITABLE ATTIRE

SUITABLE ATTIRE

Fig. 1

No sane human being would countenance leaving home on a gloomy or rainy day without a hat, a Fox-frame umbrella and a water-proof Mackintosh; and exactly the same principles of preparedness must apply to those contemplating a stint abroad. I am sure we have all witnessed, on days when torrential rain has quite clearly been forecast, a small beatnik minority who, finding themselves absent-mindedly 'caught out', can be seen scurrying for cover or trying to evade the downpour by sheltering under sodden sheets of newspaper. Similarly, there is a dangerously eccentric school of thought that advocates travelling totally unprepared. All too often bright-faced hobbledehoys and those of a bearded persuasion can be spotted on the concourses of our railway stations, seaports and aerodromes equipped only with the clothes they stand up in and a few meagre scraps of hand luggage. These people are technically known as 'fools' and it can only be hoped that they are bound for one of those ghastly Club Mating-Too-Plenty holidays or a tie-dye eco-collective, which will cater fully to their lamentable temperaments.

The Importance of Correct Dress

The first thing a traveller needs to apply his mind to is the tricky matter of correct dress. Requirements will vary enormously and, on a journey crossing several continents, could involve extremes of heat, cold, aridness and humidity calculated to turn one's bodily functions into a volatile chemistry set and one's trousers into a potential health hazard. The novice should be extremely careful to select an outfit precisely tailored to the climate and terrain he is planning to visit, as simply packing the correct assortment of garments can make all the difference between a successful adventure and hospitalisation.

A common mistake made by many a first-time traveller is to assume that he must make an effort to fit in with local customs of dress or adopt a costume that epitomises the romance of travel. The usual rationale is that if he is planning to go 'a-gipsying' then surely he must make an effort to dress like a gipsy. Cladding oneself in a ludicrous combination of bandanna, fencing shirt, velveteen knickerbockers, ammunition belt, sash and vulgar trinkets of chunky jewellery will win the respect of no one, and will more than likely attract the unwelcome attention of certain characters in questionable bars.

> In the large towns the costume of an English gentleman is the best: avoid all semi-bandit, fancy-ball extravagancies in dress; hoist, indeed, British colours there as everywhere. Thin cashmere or cubica is far preferable to cloth, which is intolerable in hot weather. Pay daily visits to Figaro, and carefully eschew the Brutus beards of La jeune France, and generally, everything which might lead the bulk of Spaniards to do you the grievous injury of mistaking your native country.
>
> *A Handbook for Travellers in Spain*, Richard Ford, 1847

In actual fact, travelling abroad should not entail any drastic diminishment of your usual dress code. As far as climate is concerned, tweed (Fig. 1) is eminently suitable for around 75 per cent

The Lost Art of Travel

of the earth's surface and, fortunately, it doubles as a badge of respectability – a sort of textile *lingua franca*. The brusque assertiveness of this cloth is usually calculated to give a traveller confidence in adversity, and to win the trust and admiration of those he meets along the way.

Temperate Zones

Most Englishmen spontaneously associate the term 'abroad' either with intense heat, dangerous insects and foul-smelling drains or, alternatively, with polar bears, crampons, and 'going outside for some time'; but the globe abounds with areas mercifully free from excesses of both heat and cold. On visiting many parts of the world, a traveller can thankfully free his mind from the dangers of perishing from dehydration or hypothermia, and should concentrate instead on such no-less-tricky dilemmas as: how to keep one's kidneys safe from a chill wind, the best material to use in handkerchief construction, or the precise design of riding trousers calculated to bypass the worst effects of saddle-chafe. With these circumstances in mind the following advice may be useful:

Nothing can surpass good heather-coloured tweed, or Waterford frieze, for ordinary wear; jackets of shooting-coat pattern, made with plenty of pockets, formed from much stronger materials than are usually made use of by tailors for that purpose, will be found more useful for knocking about in. One or two pairs of trousers may be strapped up the inside and bottom of the legs with leather, after the cavalry rough-rider pattern. The waistcoat should be cut rather long, made with four pockets, two breast and two bottom. A long loose gaberdine of woollen stuff, made to button up the front, and secured round the waist by a long narrow scarf or 'cummerbund', is an immense comfort in camp or quarters, let the climate be hot or cold. A good supply of reddish-brown socks should be laid in [Fig. 2]; a moderate number of long stockings, of the same material, to wear with the breeches; and a few dozen pairs of the 'heelless cotton' socks, for use on board ship, or when the weather is hot; nothing can be more agreeable to wear, except silk, and the cost is a mere trifle when compared to that of other hosiery. White cotton pocket-handkerchiefs, as a rule, last their owners very much longer than silk, being less tempting to native servants and followers. Braces should be always ordered of the saddler, and made from the material used for the surcingles of racehorses. There are those who dispense with braces, find great relief by the practice, and wear an ordinary waist-belt instead; but to some persons much discomfort is caused by doing so.

The best gloves for general and moderately rough usage are those sold under the name of driving gloves. They should be obtained of the regular glover, and have buckskin let in between the fingers.

Take a blue cloth pilot coat, cut long enough to reach just below the knee. The left hand breast pocket should be deep and lined with leather, as it not unfrequently becomes a resting-place for the revolver, when you do not wish to make an ostentatious display of it. Get a couple of real Scotch caps, such as the Highland shepherds wear; nothing can equal them for sleeping in.

Shifts and Expedients of Camp Life,
Lord and Baines, 1876

* * *

When exposed to the cold and piercing winds, lined and perforated chamois-leather undervests are also exceedingly efficacious; they are very light and occupy little space; and a long light comforter should not be forgotten. In warm climates a short shirt of very fine flannel, or of flannel and silk without sleeves, fitting very loosely round the neck, and reaching only as far as the hips, may be worn under a thin linen or calico shirt, while the abdomen is

Fig. 2

supported and protected by a long wide silk scarf wound two or three times round the body.

Hints to Travellers, 1883

On the basis of personal experience I cannot overemphasise the utility of the chamois-leather undervest, and for those wishing to procure such an item I can wholeheartedly recommend the services of Mr Ted Simmonds of 356a Balls Pond Road, London N1, who would be delighted to give consultation on the matter. Mr Simmonds is a highly respected window cleaner of eighteen years' standing, and when I recently had problems tracking down a vest supplier, he helpfully stepped into the breach and was more than happy to measure up Mrs Darkwood for the garment. He did a very thorough job, spending 45 minutes on the task at no extra cost, and when it came to myself he waved his hands, saying that he had 'already got the general idea', thus saving us invaluable time in our travel preparations. Now there's efficiency for you!

Of course, when talking of temperate zones, we should not necessarily assume that the traveller intends to spend his entire time roughing it. There may be occasions, and many of them, where he decides to reject the rigours of camp life and the hurly-burly of hunting game and subjugating people, in exchange for a short season attending operas, galleries and bordellos in the local cities. At such time an entirely new code of dress will apply:

A frock coat is better than a shooting jacket, which, though well enough in remote places, is strange, and will attract notice in the streets of a foreign town.

Hardships in Travel Made Easy, 1864

* * *

A capa or cloak is absolutely essential, and let it be of plain blue colour, faced with black velvet. Remember to get it made in Spain, or it will not be cut full enough to be able to be worn as the natives do; take particular care that it is a cape, dengue, esclavina, unless you wish to be an object of universal attention and ridicule.

Murray's Handbook for Travellers in Spain, 1847

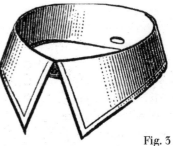

Fig. 3

When visiting civilization, it is better not to stint in the area of style. Assuming that you are only going to visit a big city for a very brief spell might tempt you to compromise your usual standards, and an unfortunate reliance on latex products may ensue. A gentleman's formal wardrobe should never contain rubber.

I take a neck-scarf to wear in the country and one rubber collar for the towns . . . The rubber collar [Fig. 3] is the pet aversion of many Englishmen but its merits for a poor traveller are obvious. Another thing which we most of us detest, a pair of elastic-sided boots, is useful in Japan, where the boots have to be kicked off before entering a house.

The Happy Traveller, Revd Frank Tatchell, 1923

Ladies' Attire

Contemporary mores seem to dictate that today's younger ladies should travel, at best, partially clothed, no matter what the weather. 'T-shirts' that are simply too short, trousers (trousers!!!) slung comically low, midriffs exposed to the elements – is it any wonder that many of them suffer terribly from kidney complaints in later life? I am no fuddy-duddy, but when it comes to ladies' fashion, what is wrong with a few floral prints, some fringes, tassels and lacy accoutrements? Surely, nothing at all.

Apart from looking dainty and becoming, a lady's clothes should also be able to bear up to the rough and ready conditions of travel (Fig. 4). This may cause a conflict of style versus practicality and durability.

Fig. 4

> The first consideration is to have every possible article made of material that can be washed – gloves, among the rest . . . Woodstock gloves (which bear washing well) are good, though, of course, they do not look very handsome. Brown holland is the best material for ladies' dresses; and nothing looks better, if set off with a little trimming of ribbon, which can be put on and taken off in a few minutes. Round straw hats, with a broad brim, such as may be had at Cairo for 4s. or 5s., are the best head covering. A double-ribbon, which bears turning when faded, will last a long time, and looks better than a more flimsy kind . . . Instead of caps, the tarboosh, when within the cabin or tent, is the most convenient, and certainly the most becoming headgear; and the little cotton cap worn under it is washed without trouble. Fans and goggles – goggles of black woven wire – are indispensable.
>
> *Eastern Life*, Harriet Martineau, 1848

Some may deride the suggestion that a lady should wear a full skirt and long sleeves in her travels, but in fact in today's world both are eminently sensible. With the advent of global warming it makes great sense to cover the arms and a long skirt prevents the harmful rays of the sun from burning the skin, as well as preventing airborne insects from alighting on the knees.

Ladies of all ages, but especially those of a certain age, such as Mrs Darkwood, who (I am sure she wouldn't mind me saying) has grown rather 'big boned' in recent years, can benefit

marvellously from some of the structured and supportive items
recommended below.

- *24 Cambric Chemise*
- *12 Cambric or Long Cloth Slips*
- *6 Middle Petticoats*
- *6 Corded Petticoats*
- *2 Corsets [Fig. 5]*
- *12 Indian Gauze or Fine Flannel Waistcoats*
- *12 Cambric Trowsers (Trimmed)*
- *24 Calico Night Dresses*
- *12 Night Caps (common)*
- *6 Mosquito trowsers for sleeping*
- *Flannel Dressing Gown (white)*
- *Coloured Flannel Dressing Gown*
- *Morning robe*
- *12 Fine French Cambric handkerchiefs [Fig. 6]*
- *6 Huckaback towels*
- *36 Diaper Towels*
- *12 Fine white cotton hose*
- *24 Lisle Thread Hose*
- *6 Lisle Thread Hose Lace Fronts*
- *2 Black silk Hose*
- *6 Riding Collars and Sleeves*
- *12 Kid gloves or silk gloves*
- *Air-Tight case for Dresses*

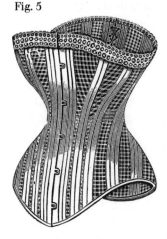

Fig. 5

Fig. 6

Murray's Handbook for Travellers in India, 1859

There is ample scientific data to show that more structured
garments are far better suited to the rigours of travel than
the flimsy clothing favoured by today's lady traveller. I have it on
good authority that galloping on horseback for days on end can
occasionally be responsible for dislodging the ovaries. A sturdy

corset, as well as lending a pleasing aesthetic to the female form, is famed for its ability to keep these safely in situ, as well as preventing the small intestine from expanding and contracting uncontrollably in rapidly fluctuating temperatures. Suitably buttressed a lady has the freedom to ride whenever she pleases.

> Ladies, who can afford the luxury, usually keep a riding horse, and provision for equestrianism should therefore be made. If morning rides only are contemplated, brown holland, grey linsey, or drab piqué riding-habits are preferable to the stereotyped black cloth garment. Those, however, who have it in view to disport themselves on horseback at the evening band-stand or other fashionable promenade, will require the usual black hat, cloth habit, etc., as worn in Hyde Park or elsewhere.
>
> *The European in India*, Edmund Hull, 1878

Mrs Darkwood is very fond of disporting herself on horseback at the bandstand. In fact she seems to be developing into quite a music lover, despite not being able to play a note. She spends many hours helping out at the military band headquarters. She maintains that there are always 101 jobs to do, ranging from making cakes and cleaning up, to giving the flugelhorn a good buffing.

Rain

As shocking as it may seem, with regard to inclement weather, a significant proportion of travel guides question the wisdom of taking an umbrella on one's peregrinations. To most Englishmen the very idea of relinquishing their trusty Smith & Sons brolly will feel like jettisoning an old friend, and abandoning all that is familiar and wholesome. In the end, I defer to individual taste but personally I would not deign to depart from Dover or Liverpool without one.

In its place various alternatives of a more or less alarming nature are proffered. The least offensive, by far, is suggested by Lord and Baines:

Fig. 7   Fig. 8

Get from some sailors' outfitter a regular seagoing sou'wester hat, with ear and neck flaps, and a pair of oiled canvas overalls to match. Procure also from a first class maker a thoroughly good India-rubber coat, long enough to come well below the tops of the butcher's boots.

Shifts and Expedients of Camp Life, Lord and Baines, 1876

Variations on this theme come in a bewildering variety. Here we illustrate just two, which whilst in my opinion no match for an umbrella can be quite fetching for both sexes (Figs. 7 & 8).

Other commentators opt for frighteningly unfamiliar articles of clothing more suited to the on-screen villains of Mr Sergio Leone than to the sons of Albion.

A poncho is very useful, for it is a sheet as well as a cloak, being simply a blanket with a slit in the middle to admit the wearer's head. A sheet of strong calico, saturated with oil, makes a waterproof poncho.

Hardships in Travel Made Easy, 1864

But the following very singular solution to keeping one's wardrobe dry in wet weather, suggested by a Mr Parkyns, must truly take the biscuit. This technique may possibly have been happened upon in the changing rooms of Charterhouse or a hammam in Marrakech (which in my opinion amounts to pretty much the same thing), and should on no account be allowed to become habitual, as such activities would be frowned upon if you were to attempt them in the environs of St James's when you finally return home.

> To keep Clothes from the wet – Mr Parkyns says, 'I may as well tell, also, how we managed to keep our clothes dry when travelling in the rain: this was rather an important consideration, seeing that each man's wardrobe consisted of what he carried on his back. Our method was at once effective and simple: if halting we took off our clothes and sat on them; if riding, they were placed under the leather shabraque of the mule's saddle, or under any article of similar material, bed or bag, that lay on the camel's pack. A good shower-bath did none of us any harm; and as soon as the rain was over, and the moisture on our skins had evaporated, we had our garments as warm, dry, and comfortable, as if they had been before a fire. In populous districts, we kept on our drawers, or supplied their place with a piece of rag, or a skin; and then, when taking off the wetted articles, hung them over the animal's cruppers to dry.'
>
> *The Art of Travel*, Francis Galton, 1872

Fig. 9

This scheme does in fact remind me of an eminently practical technique developed by Lieutenant-General Sir Henry Pemberton of the 17th Light Dragoons during the American War of Independence. In order to keep his uniform and moustache dry in inclement weather he adopted the tactics of North American Indian cattle rustlers, loosening the girth of his saddle until the shower had passed (Fig. 9).

Sundry Items

The list of extras that might be added to the very basic wardrobe outlined above is potentially endless, but there are a few requisites that it is very important not to forget. I presume the reader's common sense will prevent him from leaving England's shores without packing evening dress, smoking jacket and galoshes, but there are a few more garments he might easily overlook in the heat of departure.

Fig. 10

Gloves, Mits, and Muffs – In cold dry weather, a pair of old soft kid leather gloves, with large woollen gloves drawn over them, is the warmest combination. Mits and muffettes merely require mention. To keep the hands warm in very severe weather, a small fur muff may be slung from the neck, in which the hands may rest till wanted.

Dressing Gown – Persons who travel, even with the smallest quantity of luggage, would do wisely to take a thick dressing-gown. It is a relief to put it on in the evening, and is a warm extra dress for sleeping in. It is eminently useful, comfortable and durable [Fig. 10].

The Art of Travel, Francis Galton, 1872

* * *

Pyjamas [Fig. 11] with short gaiters are strongly recommended as the most useful things to take, and the dress can be somewhat relieved of its loose appearance by having the jacket made to button down the front and the collar a little higher than usual. It should also be fitted with breast pockets.

Fig. 11

Murray's Handbook for Travellers in Japan, 1884

The Importance of Shoes

I have left these till last, because for the traveller they are the very foundation of his kit. A badly shod man is hardly a man at all. On a journey of several months' duration he will be severely compromised if the footwear he has chosen turns out to be not up to the job. Naturally he will have made ample provision for Oxfords, patent-leather dancing pumps etc. for wear in town, but for rustic usage it is hoped he will have selected something a little more durable.

> The shoes ought to be double-soled, provided with hob nails, such as worn in shooting on England, and without iron heels, which are dangerous, and likely to slip in passing over rocks; three rows of nails are better; the weight of a shoe of this kind is counterbalanced by the effectual protection afforded to the feet against sharp rocks and loose stones, which cause contusions, and are a great source of fatigue and pain.

> *Hardships in Travel Made Easy*, 1864

Even the stoutest pair of boots (Fig. 12), given an unfavourable climate and rough terrain, will sooner or later begin to disintegrate. This is bound to happen at the least convenient moment, i.e., when a lion has just selected you as its *plat du jour*, or you have discovered an armadillo defecating on your bedding and you are preparing to give it a damned good kicking. It is perfectly possible to work your way through two or three pairs on a particularly arduous journey. In case of extreme emergencies, when your entire footwear trunk has gone up in smoke or you have been sent out into the wilds shoeless by mutinous servants, it is good to familiarise yourself with a few rudimentary techniques for constructing new shoes.

Fig. 12

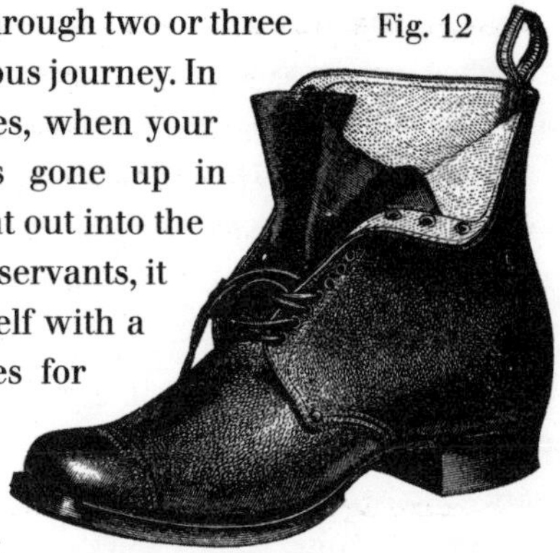

Various makeshift foot coverings are used by different nations. Some of the bushmen and half civilised Hottentots, when they have killed an animal of suitable size, such as buffalo, quagga, or any of the larger antelopes, will cut the skin all round above and below the hough, and, having stripped it off, will draw it upon their own foot, so that the heel comes where the hough of the animal used to be; the toe is then closed with a few stitches, a slit for a small tie or lancing is made on the instep, and, by walking in it before it dries or hardens, it is trodden into the shape of the foot. We have chosen the quagga skin for our illustration [Fig. 13] because the stripes help to identify the parts used for the hough-skin shoe; but it is, perhaps, the least eligible for the purpose, as it dries so hard and rigid that it must be very unpleasant to wear. The North American Indians use the hough-skin of the moose in the same manner.

Shifts and Expedients of Camp Life, Lord and Baines, 1876

Alternatively, consider involving your wife in your shoemaking activities. Co-operation of this sort not only breeds marital harmony, but also ensures extremely malleable leather:

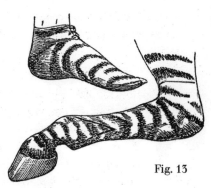

Fig. 13

The Esquimaux, after covering his feet well with birds' skins, encases them in coverings of sealskins, chewed pliant and soft by his loving spouse; over these he draws a pair of fur boots, made from the skins of bears' legs, with the feet left on.

Shifts and Expedients of Camp Life, Lord and Baines, 1876

A crisis undoubtedly obliges the traveller to act in ways that normal polite society would regard as outré in the extreme, but even if his life depends on it there are certain lines of propriety over which a traveller should never deign to step. I must remonstrate with a piece of advice given in *Hardships in Travel Made Easy*. The compiler of this work clearly states: 'Shoes of European manufacture are decidedly the best; if they wear out, and none of the party are able to make others from dressed hides, sandals may be adopted.' In a paper that I gave to the Royal Geographical Society entitled 'The Detrimental Effect of Flimsy Footwear on the Confidence and Orientation of Travellers', I laid down a hard and fast rule from which I refuse to be swayed – a gentleman never, ever wears sandals.

CHAPTER THE SECOND

Wherein Consideration is
Given to the Packing of

TRAVELLING
REQUISITES

TRAVELLING REQUISITES

Packing

The list of items to pack is not, of course, brought to a conclusion with clothing alone. There are all manner of other requisites it is essential to stow if you are to survive abroad in any comfort, and as with attire these will vary considerably according to the planned purpose of your journey. Sadly, these days

Fig. 1

the forethought given to one's essential supplies barely extends to the packing of a toothbrush, multi-plug adaptor, a roll of lavatory paper, and eight jars of Marmite. Essential as these undoubtedly are, they barely represent a hundredth of the supplies one ought to carry.

For the true traveller, the long months of preparation and planning are one of his greatest pleasures. Winter evenings will be spent polishing one's astrolabe, ensuring that one's heliograph is in full working order, and contemplating precisely how many pounds of Orange Pekoe to pack and the exact number of Sherpas or muleteers that ought to be engaged. After several drafts, a definitive supply list will be arrived at and your servants will be able to get on with the delicate and responsible task of packing.

❈

Travelling Requisites

Let some person be present at the *packing up*, as a Witness to the Contents, and make an inventory of what the trunk, &c. contains, one copy of which may be pasted inside the lid, and another kept: – the person who sees it packed should accompany it to the ware-house of the coach or wagon, and see it delivered to the book-keeper, and see it booked – therefore your porters should be able to read writing, and know what they are about; and warn them that there are plenty of rogues prowling about inn-yards, who are prodigiously polite in their offers to ease unwary porters of their luggage.

The Traveller's Oracle, Dr William Kitchiner, 1827

Indeed, rascals lurk everywhere when one is travelling and sophisticated measures should be taken to frustrate their nefarious activities at every turn.

Closely-fitted well-made cases afford great trouble to thieves, and gaping packages, with partly exposed contents, invite robbery. Boxes which are *screwed* down are more secure than nailed boxes, as thieves are frequently not provided with screwdrivers.

Hints to Travellers, Douglas W. Freshfield and
Captain W.J. Wharton, 1889

In these times of global terrorism and international drug smuggling, a salutary tale might alert potential travellers to the dire circumstances that can ensue if one inadequately secures one's luggage or leaves it unattended. A Mr Simm of Edinburgh, related to me the following story: 'I was residing for a short while at the South African farmstead of Lady Anaglypta Beest (last in a long line of Beests responsible for the early colonization of the Transvaal). At the end of my visit, as I was preparing to take my leave of the noble Lady, she gathered together her small menagerie of cats and small creatures of the Veldt to see me off, but was very much distressed that her pet Chihuahua, Terreblanche, was nowhere to be found. She feared that the little mite had been taken by hyenas. It was only after my return home that the truth emerged. The unfortunate dog had crawled into my luggage through a small gap left by a damaged clasp and was found curled up in my toiletry bag, asphyxiated, his head firmly lodged in my shaving mug.' Nothing could be more instructive to the modern traveller, never to leave his luggage in a state of unreadiness and always to double-check its contents before departure.

Fig. 2

The Shaving Mug – even the most innocuous of items can become a danger whilst abroad.

Customs Officials

Customs officials are pretty much the same the world over – jumped-up flunkies with an inexplicably high opinion of themselves; but to glide smoothly around the globe it is important to hold one's tongue and attempt to deal with them with politeness and courtesy (supplemented with a liberal application of baksheesh). But, despite your largesse, never assume that a border guard is 'in your pocket', because as soon as you turn your back that is precisely where you will find him rummaging around.

> Travellers should never permit Custom-House Officers to examine two trunks at the same time – while the owner's eye and attention are fixed on one, the other may be pillaged.
>
> *The Traveller's Oracle*, Dr William Kitchiner, 1827

As a rule, customs staff will go out of their way to kick up a fuss about every trifling infringement of border regulations. In today's world climate, especially if flying, it might be diplomatic to draw their attention towards any commodities that you harbour doubts about.

> Chemicals and explosives should be kept separate from other things; and, before being packed, inquiry should be made as to regulations to which they will have to submit on ship-board, &c. If the goods have to undergo customs examination, the traveller must be present himself, or he risks the goods being disarranged and carelessly repacked, and the eatables extensively tested by tasting.
>
> *Hints to Travellers*, Douglas W. Freshfield and Captain W.J. Wharton, 1889

Despite one's best efforts, the skulduggery of servants or a slight oversight on one's own part can lead to embarrassment. Ignorant of the Englishman's innate sense of fair play, foreign customs officials are bound to attribute to one the same low moral standards as their fellow countrymen possess, and will read criminal intent even into seemingly innocuous articles.

> A traveller should also strictly forbid his servant carrying contraband goods; because, in case of detection, the master would very probably lose his luggage, and most certainly suffer a very unpleasant detention.
>
> With regard to the inconvenience arising from taking contraband luggage, I unfortunately, in the hurry of packing for the Continent, put, among others, three cotton night caps into my portmanteau, which had neither been worn or washed. On entering the King of Sardinia's Dominions, at a place called Beauvoisin, they were instantly pounced upon as prohibited articles; and it was with the greatest difficulty and trouble, after much delay and loss of time, that my companions could induce the Douaniers to believe that they were articles requisite for a traveller, and that the heinous crime of smuggling was foreign to our thoughts.
>
> *The Traveller's Oracle*, Dr William Kitchiner, 1827

27

Personal Effects

There are some quite eminent explorers who preach against packing what they regard as too many chattels and err on the side of travelling alarmingly light. Frankly, I am not sure I am able to see the wisdom of this. I am inclined to follow William Kitchiner's far more sensible advice, 'Those who travel for pleasure must not disquiet their minds with

Fig. 3

A beast of burden is never happier than when it is given a useful occupation by man

the cares of too great economy, or, instead of pleasure, they will find nothing but vexation', and pack accordingly (Fig. 3). There will of course be a limit to the amount you are able to take, based on the number of servants (staff shortages are always the bane of a traveller) and the modes of transport that are available to you, but generally speaking, for a party of four, you should pack no more than you can conveniently fit onto eighteen pack horses, a small pantechnicon or medium bi-plane.

The list of a traveller's personal effects is potentially limitless and to a great extent will depend upon individual preference, but a brief guide might be useful. My personal recommendations include: coat hangers and shoe-trees; a portable dressing-case (Fig. 4) containing grooming paraphernalia such as hair brushes, comb, nail brush, Pomade Hongrois moustache wax, tooth brushes, scissors, Macassar hair oil, portable looking glass; a sink plug on a chain (rarely found in foreign countries); magnifying glass and flower press; fly whisk; golf

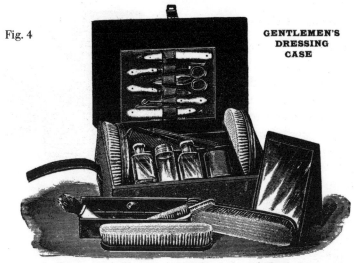

Fig. 4

**GENTLEMEN'S
DRESSING
CASE**

No. 7. With strap and buckle, lock and key, leather divisions, case lined leather, containing 2 hair brushes, hat, cloth, tooth, nail and shaving brushes, screw powder jar, 2 square scent bottles, soap case, metal case for tooth brush, comb, strop, 2 razors, scissors, button hook, nail file, tweezers, mirror. Size, 11¾ by 8 by 3¾ in.
In solid brown leather ... 80/0 | In pigskin............... 87/0 | In crocodile 98/0

clubs and cricket gear; pocket sundial; a bag of cleft sticks for sending messages; and miniature cannon (for saluting the Queen on her birthday) (Fig. 5). To these may be added the following:

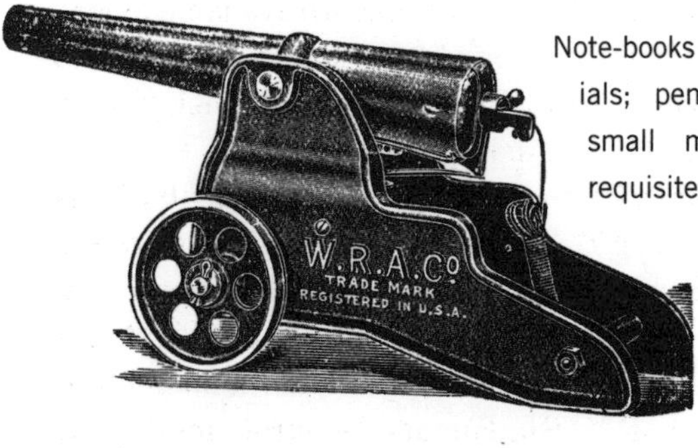

Note-books and writing materials; pencils; cigars; flask; small medicine chest or requisite medicines; knife; shoehorn; extra boot laces (hippopotamus hide are best); patent grease for boots; compass; aneroid. A gun – if a revolver [Fig. 6] is

Fig. 5 *A small saluting gun is essential for commemorating the Queen's birthday, Trafalgar Day and the beginning of the grouse season*

29

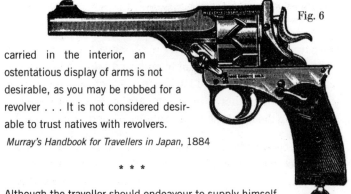

Fig. 6

carried in the interior, an
ostentatious display of arms is not
desirable, as you may be robbed for a
revolver . . . It is not considered desirable to trust natives with revolvers.

Murray's Handbook for Travellers in Japan, 1884

* * *

Although the traveller should endeavour to supply himself
with books that are worth reading and re-reading, still, it is
astonishing with what pleasure he will peruse the veriest rubbish
in the wilderness, and really crave for anything that may serve to dis-
tract his mind at times from the savagery around him.

Hints to Travellers, Douglas W. Freshfield and
Captain W.J. Wharton, 1889

Happily disassociated from the problematic arena of his
wardrobe, a gentleman traveller can reassess the acceptability of
latex products and even allow them to insinuate themselves into
his luggage without any accompanying sense of shame.

An India-rubber cushion is invaluable; it serves as a pillow by night,
and eases the jolting of the carriole by day.

*Murray's Handbook for Travellers in Denmark,
Norway, Sweden, and Iceland*, 1858

* * *

An India rubber bath, with bellows to distend it, is an immense
comfort, though a serious addition to weight [Fig. 7].

Murray's Handbook for Travellers in Greece, 1884

Other items may not suggest themselves immediately, but you
will soon discover that some commodities regarded as commonplace at home may prove scarce whilst travelling abroad.

Soap is indispensable, being a rare article on the Continent.

Hardships in Travel Made Easy, 1864

Over twenty-five years of travel experience I have rarely found any commodity more adaptable and useful than a knobbly stick. As we will see later, a well-selected buckthorn is an invaluable tool for, among other things, pitching tents, digging wells, and persuading the locals as to the validity of your point of view.

A stout buckthorn stick, as a weapon of defence, three feet in length, on which may be marked the inches and thus serve as a measure.

Hardships in Travel Made Easy, 1864

Those wanting to cut more of a dash, perhaps in a sincere but misguided emulation of Mr Errol Flynn, will probably opt for a sword-stick instead.

Sword and *Tuck Sticks*, as commonly made, are hardly so good a weapon as a stout stick – the blades are often inserted into the handles in such a slight manner, that one smart blow will break them out – if you wish for a *Sword-Cane*, you must have one made with a good Regulation Blade, which alone will cost more than is usually charged for the entire stick – I have seen a cane made by Mr. Price, *of the Stick and Umbrella Warehouse, No. 221 in the Strand*, which was excellently put together.

The Traveller's Oracle, Dr William Kitchiner, 1827

Fig. 7

30 by 8 in.	39/9	Cases for do.	3/2
36 „ 8 „	47/9	Bellows for do.	4/7

Inflating Baths (Circular).

Whilst a sword-cane has no significant advantage over the knobbly stick in repelling a foe, it does have the edge when it comes to impressing servants, business colleagues and, especially, the ladies. My colleague the incorrigible Colonel Pearce has frequently held sway over the breakfast table by halving grapefruit and catapulting toast from the toast rack using his foil. I have witnessed serving maids, and the usually level-headed Mrs Darkwood, literally swoon at his vigorous lungings into the devilled kidney dish.

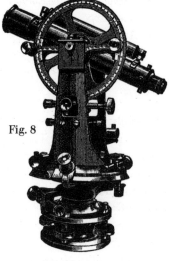

Fig. 8

Scientific Instruments and Other Gadgets

A great deal of time overseas will be spent measuring things, collecting specimens, charting coasts, surveying ruins and making trigonometric calculations of the height of celestial bodies etc. A wide array of precision-engineered instruments will be required to carry out this work. I hope I am not insulting readers' intelligence by reminding them to pack such obvious items as a barograph, theodolite (Fig. 8), sextant, anemometer, clay pigeon catapult (Fig. 9), and a Stuart's Marine Distance Meter. These can be supplemented as follows:

Fig. 9 *The Clay Pigeon Catapult – a good way of keeping your eye in if things prove slow on the exotic bird front*

- *A thermometer, this may be in a tooth-pick case.*

Travelling Requisites

- A barometer for measuring heights, this may be in a walking-stick.
- A telescope, a microscope [Fig. 10], an opera-glass.
- A knife containing a large and small blade, a saw, hook for taking stones out of a horse's foot, turnscrew, gun-picker, tweezers, and a corkscrew long and large enough to be useful.

Hardships in Travel Made Easy, 1864

Personally, despite the views of some experts who regard them as irretrievably amateur, I am not averse to the multi-tool penknife. A Swiss Army Knife is as much a state of mind as it is a practical tool. Even if your destination is a tour of the galleries of Florence, where (unless you have hatched a plan to relieve some of the picture-frames of their contents) it will be of minimal use, the mere presence of this handy accoutrement in your jacket pocket will confer a sense of safety and wellbeing. It is a totem of supreme readiness, and knowing that at any given moment you can spring into action to relieve a lame horse of its gravel-clogged hoof, de-hook a fish from a recalcitrant barb or liberate the contents of a bottle of Châteauneuf du Pape will allow you always to walk with your head held high.

Fig. 10

Another focus of unwarranted snobbery is the use of too many novel gadgets, but always remember that one man's absolute necessity is another man's waste of space. I completely acknowledge that satellite navigation systems, short-band radios, radar, pocket calculators and the like are the worst sort of frippery and only serve to take the challenge and fun out of exploration; but who can seriously question the value of a typewriter, mangle, travel loom, camera obscura, wind-up gramophone (Fig. 11) and Aldis lamp? I would simply have refused to believe that experienced explorers would go so far as to criticise the use of a canteen if I had not seen it here with my own two eyes:

"MONARCH" SENIOR GRAMOPHONE.

Fig. 11

Oak cabinet. Triple spring motor. 12 in. turntable. Speed indicator. "Morning Glory" Horn.

Each £11 0 0

> Do not on any account be induced to encumber your-self with a 'canteen'. It would be impossible to teach a native cook how to use them, and it would be easier to give him a fathom of calico to buy half-a-dozen earthen pots, and to buy more when these were broken. It is, no doubt, vastly ingenious to make a pepper-dredge fit into a tea-canister which belongs in the tea pot, which in turn should go into the saucepan, only unfortunately the class of person to whom utensils of this kind are usually entrusted in wild countries are slow to appreciate mechanical puzzles, and usually throw the whole lot into the first bag they can get, when the spout of the teapot gets knocked off, and the pepper becomes hopelessly amalgamated with the tea, to the decided detriment of both.

Shifts and Expedients of Camp Life, Lord and Baines, 1876

Tools

A rudimentary tool set is essential for all but the most sedentary of travels. Living for weeks in the outback or setting up base camp at the foot of a mountain range, it may be necessary to construct a rude hut. You will, no doubt, have employed men extremely pro-ficient in the use of saws, hammers, bradawls and the like, and they should be able to fabricate a suitable dwelling in about three hours – one hour to erect the structure and the other two to carve the detailing on the veranda, eaves, corbels, pediments and finials.

A few tools, well selected, can scarcely be dispensed with:
- *A strong well-made Butcher's knife*
- *Small hand axe, felling axe (American pattern)*
- *Belt tomahawk*
- *Hand saw (medium size)*
- *Three chisels (¾in., ½in., and ¼in.)*
- *Three gouges (of the same sizes as the chisels)*
- *Three gimblets (from ten-penny nail size downwards)*
- *Six bradawls (assorted), to fit in one boxwood handle*
- *Six saddler's awls*
- *Six shoemaker's awls*
- *One ½in. shell auger (without handle)*
- *One screw driver*
- *One engineer's riveting hammer (½lb.)*
- *One pair of carpenter's pincers*
- *One pair of strong pliers (bell-hanger's pattern)*
- *Three hand saw files (one rat-tail; one flat; one half-round)*
- *One rasp, one soldering bolt, one pair of tin snips, ingot of solder, a lump of resin, and small ladle for lead melting*
- *Bill hook*

Shifts and Expedients of Camp Life, Lord and Baines, 1876

In addition to the above you may want to consider packing an angle grinder, various sizes of mason's chisels, block and tackle, and a pneumatic road drill. There is a long-standing British tradition of bringing back souvenirs and knick-knacks from overseas, and you will not be taken seriously as a traveller unless you return with a few crates of antiquities to display in a room, named after you, in the British Museum. Archaeological relics are often inconveniently embedded in the ground or attached to structures far too big to export, so a good range of stone-cutting equipment is absolutely essential (Fig. 12).

But a note of caution. The first (and last) time I travelled with Mr Helios's Easyplane, my butcher's knife, rat-tail hand-saw and entire collection of bradawls were unaccountably confiscated. Circumvent such bureaucracy by carrying such divers ironmongery in a sturdy portmanteau checked-in in advance of the flight, and not, as I did, in a figure-hugging 'Steeplejack' multi-tool vest (available from selected branches of Tools-R-Us). Being wrestled to the floor by three burly security guards as I walked through the metal detector seemed a disproportionate response to a perfectly natural misunderstanding. My subsequent terrorisation with a rubber glove in an adjacent booth further convinced me that the sedentary pen pushers and petty officials of this world will always resent the man of action whom they secretly envy and admire.

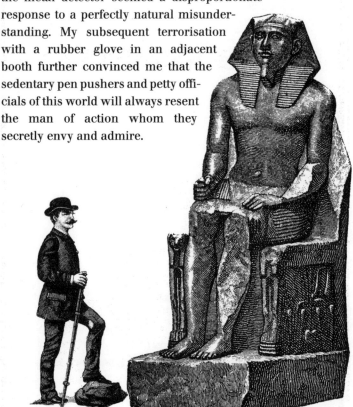

Fig. 12 *Unless a traveller returns home bearing a few suitable gift items he runs the risk of being seen as parsimonious by colleagues and friends*

CHAPTER THE THIRD

Outlining the Best Methods of Securing

FOOD SUPPLIES

FOOD SUPPLIES

As you set out towards the nearest aerodrome or seaport, maybe by motor-car, or, more stylishly, cantering down the open highway with a retinue of servants and packhorses, you are unlikely to make it even as far as the Clacket Lane Services before it dawns on you that, as Napoleon observed, 'an army marches on its stomach'. Meagre or sub-standard provisions will rapidly sow discontent amongst your bearers and travel companions, and unless you want ultimately to find yourself set adrift in a boat on the high seas or left to perish tied to a Baobab tree, you had better ensure there are adequate provisions for all. A professional explorer knows that there are only three possible sources for these victuals: those bought from Fortnum & Mason or other grocer of repute prior to departure; those procured from vendors, locals and swarthy innkeepers en route; and, finally, the 'free' sustenance bagged by him from bountiful Nature in the form of animals, plants and scavenged 'survival food'.

Fig. 1 *A traveller may experience a sense of grief at having to leave behind all that he holds most dear*

Food Supplies

Provisions to Pack

One of the greatest privations a traveller suffers when going abroad is
estrangement from the food items
that he holds most dear. It is unwise
to allow your mind to dwell too
heavily on this matter in the days
leading up to your departure, as such
maudlin introspection is only calculated to have you waking up in the
middle of the night, in a cold sweat,
stammering delirious paeans to eggs
Benedict, jam roly-poly and Nanny
Bridlington's delectable meat pies
(Fig. 1). It has to be admitted that

Fig. 2

even if you are well provided with packhorses, porters, or even,
where roads exist, a motor-car, the sheer perishability of such
foodstuffs will usually rule them off any provisions list, and a
grisly assortment of preserved comestibles may have to take their
place:

> The following are recommended as the most useful things to take,
> and if the plan of sending relays to different places be adopted, the
> luggage need never be inconveniently heavy:
> Liebig's Extract of Beef; German pea-soup sausage; Chicago Corned
> Beef; Tinned Milk; Biscuits; Jam; Cheese; Salt and Mustard;
> Worcestershire Sauce; Bacon; and Tea and Sugar.
>
> *Murray's Handbook for Travellers in Japan*, 1884

* * *

> Maccaroni, Harvey sauce, mustard, pepper, basket-salt, arrowroot,
> preserved meats, portable soups, hams, and dried tongues are useful,
> and absolutely necessary for those who travel in places where meat
> is not to be procured.
>
> *Murray's Handbook for Travellers in Constantinople*, 1871

❋

The Lost Art of Travel

* * *

The following are good for all countries and all climates: tea (in tins); Liebig's extract (sold usually in jars, but will keep equally in well-soldered tins); preserved soups in tins (Symington's pea-flour soup is excellent at low temperatures, and requires only one minute's boiling); lemonade effervescing powder (will keep perfectly if soldered in tin); dried onions; eating-raisins; chocolate in cakes; mustard, salt, pepper and curry-powder.

Hints to Travellers, 1883

Those simply unable to contemplate days, let alone weeks, spent surviving on such humdrum fare might consider taking with them a portable calor gas refrigerator made by Ditchling and Fobb of Market Rasen, fitted with pack-saddle attachment and Sherpatex® shoulder straps. But unless life is unimaginable without it, the traveller is probably better off dispensing with such an item. On the one occasion that we experimented with it, on an ascent of Machu Picchu, the ungainly weight of the contraption resulted in one of our porters losing his footing and tumbling 300 yards down the mountainside. We naturally raced down the hill to see if there was anything to be done, but tragically not one of the bottles of Veuve Clicquot that it contained had survived intact and the refrigerator was beyond repair.

In any case, in colder climates the preservation of foodstuffs becomes less of an issue. When William Hawes and Charles Fellows made an ascent of Mont Blanc in 1827, they packed food supplies of much more satisfying calibre and far more calculated to set the mountain air alight with sparkling postprandial badinage.

They carried with them five pounds and a half of cheese, eight large loaves, eight pieces of meat, eleven fowls, twenty seven bottles of vin ordinaire, two bottles of Bordeaux, two of cognac, two of eau de cerise, fourteen of sirop de framboise, capellaire, and lemonade; lemons, raisins and prunes.

A Narrative of an Ascent to the Summit of Mont Blanc, Benjamin Hawes, 1828

Food Supplies

Fig. 3

All in all, the group leader will come to his own conclusions as to which provisions are most calculated to keep up morale. My general rule of thumb is that for a journey of three months you should pack the bare minimum for survival – say, around seven hampers per head containing such comforting staples as: stuffed olives; Wilkston's Piccalilli; waxed truckles of Shropshire blue; Henderson's 'brandy-drowned' Dormouse with Hazelnuts (in jars); and chocolate HobNobs.

Locally Sourced Victuals

The received wisdom is that outside Paris and discreet pockets in St Petersburg, Casablanca, Monte Carlo and Singapore, all foreign food is utterly atrocious, and this for the most part turns out to be perfectly true. In countries free from efficient transport, rudimentary hygiene and refrigeration it may be necessary to become accustomed to (and even begin to appreciate) authentic peasant fare, i.e., food that is stale, mouldy and full of weevils.

Unfortunately, writer and social campaigner Harriet Martineau was not prepared to have any truck with local delicacies during her visit to the Middle East in 1848, but was less suspicious of indulging in the joys of the native pipe. It seems that in Syria, as in some areas of Glasgow, a diet that eschews solids in favour of plenty of liquids and tobacco products is the best way of promoting good health in a land of questionable culinary skills.

As to diet – our party are all of opinion that it is the safest way to eat and drink as nearly as possible as one does at home. It may be worth mentioning that the syrups and acids which some travellers think they shall like in the Desert are not wholesome, nor so refreshing as might

41

Fig. 4

be anticipated. Ale and porter are much better – as remarkably wholesome and refreshing as they are at sea. Tea and coffee are pleasant everywhere. Ladies who have courage to do what is good for them, and agreeable to them, in new circumstances, in disregard of former prejudices, will try the virtues of the chibouque [Fig. 4] while in the East; and if they like it, they will go on with it as long as they feel that they want it. The chibouque would not be in such universal use as it is in the East, if there were not some reason for it; and the reason is that it is usually found eminently good for health.

Eastern Life, Harriet Martineau, 1848

It does not do to be too high-handed or condescending when judging the lamentably comic efforts made by foreign chefs. One must show compassion and make allowances, as one does with children and the mentally deficient. Sadly, fellow commentators sometimes fail to see things this way and are all too ready to slander the best efforts of their hosts left, right and centre.

Caution Regarding Food taken in the Tropics – Every new comer to a warm climate should be particularly careful to observe moderation and simplicity in his diet. The newly arrived European should content himself with a plain breakfast of bread and butter, with tea or coffee, without indulging in meat, fresh eggs, or buttered toast. The butter alone often disagrees and occasions rancidity, with nausea, while it increases the secretion of bile, already in excess. The dirty habits of the native cooks, who will be often seen buttering toast with the greasy wing of a fowl, or an old dirty piece of rag, will perhaps be of more avail than any medical caution in inducing Europeans to give up this injurious article of food.

Hardships in Travel Made Easy, 1864

* * *

[In Portugal] the question is frequently not between good and bad food, but between eating and going without. Among other things, unless the traveller means to live on black bread, he must be careful to take a good supply of white. However, in ordinary country *estalagens*, eggs may generally be procured in any number for about 2*d*. the dozen. As, of course, egg-cups or spoons are out of the question, it is best to have them boiled (*ovos cozidos*). Chickens (*frangos*) and hens (*gallinhas*) are sometimes procurable, but always resemble leather. Although tea (*chà*) is quite a national drink, it is such an infusion as an Englishman would hardly taste.

Murray's Handbook for Travellers in Portugal, 1855

* * *

A friend of mine, who in addition to his passionate devotion to *la chasse*, possessed the keenest affection for his dinner, assured me, once upon a time, that *good bread* was the back-bone of happiness – gustatory happiness that is to say – in the jungle. In cantonment even, this man despised the miserable travesty called bread by the native baker – they say he once *saw it being made*, never thought of it again without a shudder, and preferred a home-made roll for ever afterwards.

Culinary Jottings for Madras, A.R. Kenney-Herbert, 1883

In light of the above, a timorous diner may conclude that a wholly vegetarian diet, whatever it may lack in terms of gustatory satisfaction, will at least pose no danger to health. Unhappily, like many of the assumptions one makes whilst abroad, this is not necessarily the case, and a great amount of discernment is required in choosing between items which are safe and those which are likely to buy you a one-way ticket to the intensive care unit or mortuary.

Raw vegetables, such as cucumbers, and salads, and most fruits, are to be eschewed. The abundance of fruit is often a temptation, but nothing is more pernicious, or more likely to lead to fatal consequences. Melons are generally to be shunned: the plants being usually irrigated with tank or other stagnant water, this fruit is a frequent and unsuspected cause of fever [Fig. 5].

Murray's Handbook for Travellers in Greece, 1884

Fig. 5 *A useful mnemonic for reinforcing sensible attitudes towards injurious vegetables whilst abroad*

* * *

Particular types of fruit have particular effects on certain constitutions; thus *mangoes* have sometimes a stimulating and heating effect, which often bring out pustules and boils on the unseasoned European. The *pine apple*, though very delicious, is not a safe fruit at any time. The *orange* is always grateful and wholesome, as is the *shaddock*, owing to its cooling subacid qualities. The *banana* is wholesome and nutritious, whether undressed or cooked.

Murray's Handbook for Travellers in India, 1859

But ultimately, a traveller should not assume that all food abroad is *totally* beneath contempt *always* and *everywhere*. It is more a case of taking time to acclimatise the palate to the peculiarities of the indigenous dishes, and the digestive tract to the seething mass of bacteria and microbes that, in hot climes, reside in all local fare. When travelling the Englishman should expect to relax his attitudes towards much which at home he would regard as foetid, unhygienic, unwholesome, vile or depraved. As time passes, Nanny Bridlington will become but a dim and distant memory, and the more you experiment, the braver you will become in partaking of the local delicacies.

I have myself dined on unusual dishes across the globe: raw breast of puffin and guillemot in Iceland; the still-beating heart of the cobra in Vietnam (Fig. 6); the potentially deadly fugu fish in Japan; Bagoong from the Philippines, Surströmming from Sweden, Criadillas from Spain and apart from the trifling episode that called for the use of a makeshift stomach/bicycle pump in Rangoon, I feel I have gained nothing but benefit from the experience. Sometimes it is the mere sound of dishes that excites the interest. Mr Kenney-Herbert in his *Culinary Jottings for Madras* contrives an impressive list: 'Cocoanut oil, pish pash, conjee water, ghee, buffado, chepatties, ding dong, country captain, ramakin toast, and washerman's pie!' I am yet to ascertain the precise ingredients of 'ding dong', but if any reader would care to furnish me with a list of ingredients, I should be immensely grateful.

When unfamiliar dishes and cooking techniques are imported to our own shores, it is sometimes easier to appreciate them. Observing exotic culinary methods practised in the reassuring surroundings of a 135-acre estate in Huntingdonshire, for example, it is possible to cease eyeing them with the suspicion they aroused when first encountered outside a one-room shack overseas:

Fig. 6

Novel Method of Cooking a Shoulder of Mutton – When Omai, a chief of the Sandwich Islands, was staying at the house of Lord Sandwich, at

Hinchinbrook, it was proposed that he should cook a shoulder of mutton in his own manner, at which he was quite delighted. Having dug a deep hole in the ground, he placed fuel at the bottom of it, and then covered it with clean pebbles; when properly heated, he laid the mutton, neatly enveloped in leaves, at the top, and having closed the hole, walked constantly round it, very deliberately observing the sun. The meat was afterwards brought to the table, and was found to be excellently cooked. This improvisation of a culinary apparatus may serve as a hint for travellers placed in a similar position.

Hardships in Travel Made Easy, 1864

A young adventurer who acquires a modest repertoire of exotic recipes will discover that he is much in demand when he returns to the old country. Inviting friends around for an evening of sloth-toe pâté, roast kinkajou and durian syllabub will make you the talk of the town. As Galton observes: 'It is no slight advantage to a young man, to have the opportunity for distinction which travel affords. If he plans his journey among scenes and places likely to interest the stay-at-home public, he will probably achieve a

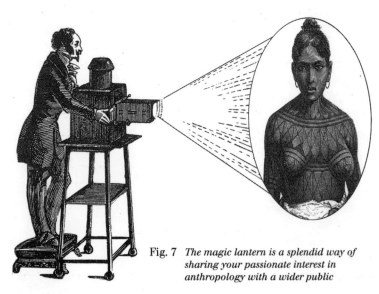

Fig. 7 *The magic lantern is a splendid way of sharing your passionate interest in anthropology with a wider public*

reputation that might well be envied by wiser men who have not had his opportunities.'

Planning a series of endangered-species supper evenings entailing exotic bird impersonations, a magic lantern presentation (Fig. 7) and a display of lithesome dancing from your personal nautch-girl troupe will have the whole of the western world, bar a few po-faced conservationists, beating down your door to attend, and will lend you the romantic appeal of a T.E. Lawrence or a Byron, no doubt placing at your lubricious disposal the entire typing pool at the Royal Geographical Society.

But be careful. Nutritionally, foreign food is an unknown quantity. Whilst our native pies and puddings lovingly crafted from suet, sugar and lard are eminently good for health, an over-indulgence in unfamiliar foreign dishes may have unforeseen circumstances. The following extract may act as a warning:

> The truth is, that Hindostannee fops (and most of the superior orders are such) pride themselves above all things, on rotundity of corporation, and particularly on the magnitude of their heads. To acquire such elegant distinction, one would be tempted to suspect, that they occasionally broke the vegetable regime, and indulged in better fare than Brahma thought proper to prescribe. But no; all is accomplished by ghee and indolence! Of the former, which is a kind of semi-liquid butter, made by evaporating the aqueous part of the rich milk of the buffalo, they swill immense quantities; and whatever we may hear, from fireside travellers, of Hindoo temperance and abstemiousness, these gentry contrive to become as bilious, occasionally, as their European neighbours.
>
> *The Influence of Tropical Climates on European Constitutions,*
> James Johnson, 1815

Emergency Rations

Even on the most meticulously planned expedition circumstances can sometimes go nastily awry without the slightest hint of warning, and the independent traveller will be brought perilously close to disaster. Unforeseen misfortunes such as the camp's sous-chef and pastry-cook being eaten by army ants, the town you were heading for turning out to be a figment of a disgruntled carto-grapher's imagination, or finding yourself separated from the group after wandering off in pursuit of an Owsten's Palm Civet, are just some of the more routine events that are liable to happen on any journey. You will suddenly find yourself hungry and vulnerable, possibly quite alone, and will have to fall back on your own resources in order to survive. It is recommended that you acquire some tried and tested techniques for finding and prepar-ing emergency rations that will keep you nour-ished until a search party arrives or you are adopted as a demi-god by a native tribe. New Age techniques designed to keep you safe through harmony with the natural world, such as trying to imbue yourself with the spirit of the leopard or chanting the mantras of Krishna, will be of precious little use, and a hungry big cat will probably have your legs off by the time you have uttered your second 'Hare Rama'. Likewise, the error of assuming that you know everything you need to know about bushcraft because you watched the entire video box-set of Ray Mears' *World of Survival* one wet weekend in October will only become apparent when you are racking your brain to remember whether it was the red tree frog that was nutritious and the green tree frog deadly poisonous, or vice versa.

Fig. 8

Even if a traveller lacks the where-withal or know-how to stride out and hunt for game (see later section), *in extremis* he can at least survive using a wealth of freely available natural nutriments, and, failing that, unlikely-seeming items from his own wardrobe.

Food for Travellers from Various Sources – There are two nutritious plants, nettle and fern, that are found in many countries. Respecting these, the following extract from Messrs. Hue and Gabet's travels may be of service: 'When the young stems of ferns are gathered quite tender, before they are covered with down, and while the first leaves are bent and rolled upon themselves, you have only to boil them in pure water to realise a dish of delicious asparagus [Fig. 8]. We would also recommend the nettle, which in our opinion might be made an advantageous substitute for spinach; indeed we proved this more than once by our own experience.

Most kinds of creeping things are eatable, and used by the Chinese. Locusts and grasshoppers are not at all unwholesome. To prepare them, pull off the legs and wings, and roast them with a little grease in an iron dish. Rank sea-birds, if caught, put in a coop, and fed with corn, will become fat and well-tasted.'

Hardships in Travel Made Easy, 1864

* * *

As to hunger, a man can live on his own fat for a week and it is a poor country where there are no lichens. These boiled for an hour will keep you going, and it is useful to know that no toadstool growing on a tree is poisonous. If you have any food left when you first realise that you have lost your way, save it until nightfall and eat half of it when you camp. In the morning only have a drink and eat your last food at midday. After that, drink only a sip at a time and chew pieces of your boots. Water above house-level is sure to be pure and good to drink.

The Happy Traveller, Revd Frank Tatchell, 1923

* * *

Revolting Food, that may save the Lives of Starving Men:
Carrion is not noxious to Starving Men – In reading the accounts of travellers who have suffered severely from want of food, a striking fact

is common to all, that, under those circumstances, carrion and garbage of every kind can be eaten without the stomach rejecting it. Life can certainly be maintained on a revolting diet that would cause a dangerous illness to a man who was not compelled to adopt it by the pangs of hunger.

Skins – All old hides or skins of any kind that are not tanned are fit and good for food; they improve soup by being mixed with it; or they may be toasted and hammered. Many a hungry person has cooked and eaten his sandals or skin clothing.

Bones contain a great deal of nourishment, which is got at by boiling them, pounding their ends between two stones, and sucking them. There is a revolting account in French history, of a besieged garrison of Sancerre, in the time of Charles IX, and again subsequently at Paris, and it may be elsewhere, digging up the grave-yards for bones as sustenance.

Blood from Live Animals – The Aliab tribe, who have great herds of cattle on the White Nile, 'not only milk their cows, but they bleed their cattle periodically, and boil the blood for food. Driving a lance into a vein in the neck, they bleed the animals copiously, which operation is repeated about once a month.' (Sir S. Baker) [Fig. 9].

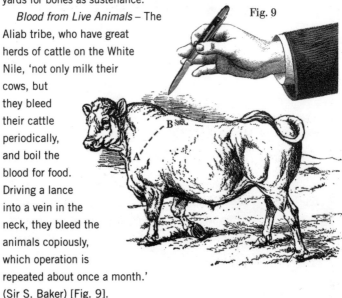

Fig. 9

The Art of Travel, Francis Galton, 1872

CHAPTER THE FOURTH

On the Location and Imbibing of

WATER AND OTHER BEVERAGES

WATER AND OTHER BEVERAGES

Water

At home on his country estate, an Englishman can sometimes become a little blasé about the availability of a good-quality water supply. One turn of the tap provides limitless gallons for the duties of his laundresses, cooks, stable lads and scullery maids; his daily ablutions; the filling of his ornamental duck pond; the maintenance of the croquet lawn; and the irrigation of the orchid house. A tendency to take water for granted is

Fig. 1

exacerbated by the fact that on British soil, water as a quencher of thirst, has never been regarded with much enthusiasm. A gentleman rarely if ever permits water to pass his lips in its pure unadulterated state, preferring, as he does, the far more stimulating and refreshing effects of 1990 Dom Pérignon, mulligatawny soup, lapsang souchong, or the seemingly endless variety of concoctions invented by Leonard, the in-house cocktail waiter (Fig. 1).

Abroad, the insufferable rigours of the trail are likely to force a traveller to modify his prejudices and behaviour; and he may be startled to find, for the first time in his life, that water suggests itself as a perfectly viable, and even desirable, beverage. The sad irony is that no sooner does pristine H_2O become attractive to the palate than it also proves horribly difficult to come by. In Arctic regions all fresh water is in its solid state; in the Tropics it is generally foetid and laced with dead cats and human effluent; in deserts, with the exception of a few picturesquely appointed oases, it is virtually non-existent. Only on the lower slopes of mountainous regions where crystal-clear streams wend their way down from snow-covered peaks can a traveller set out with much confidence in a clean and ready supply.

Therefore, in much the same way as demonstrated in the previous chapter on foodstuffs, an adventurer will have to decide how much and which varieties of fluid matter he will carry with him, and what he feels it is safe to source along the way. This decision will be based on knowledge of your destination, but will chiefly revolve around how lucky you feel. It is foolish to suppose that just because you intend to confine your travels to countries that might be regarded as broadly westernised, you will not be faced with irregular water supplies and resultant alimentary grief.

Caution against drinking water in Holland – In the provinces of Holland, bordering on the sea, the water is generally bad; indeed, not fit to drink; and strangers should be careful to avoid it altogether, except for the purposes of ablution, or they will most probably be attacked with bowel complaints, and be delayed in their journey.

Hardships in Travel Made Easy, 1864

* * *

The water found in the country is apt to be charged with matter, which produces deleterious effects upon the stomach of a foreigner. The heat increases one's thirst by producing perspiration, and the only remedy to this is tea, for there is nothing so effectual in allaying thirst.

Murray's Handbook for Travellers in Constantinople, 1871

As we will see later, tea may be regarded as the saviour of the water-drinker, but in its absence the traveller will need to exert extreme caution wherever he goes, and especially in the Tropics. One minute he might be chatting to the Viceroy on the verandah of the Embassy, sipping an innocuous glass of chilled water; the next, flat on his back attended by his punkah wallah and maids staving off the worst effects of swamp fever. He should therefore ascertain the purity of the water he consumes and ensure that it has been prepared carefully:

> The habit of drinking large draughts of iced water, so common in India, when the body is heated, or during meals, is often attended with mischief, and always with risk to the stomach or other of the abdominal organs. Such water should be taken in small quantities at a time, or even slowly sipped. Water used for drinking or cooking purposes should always be filtered through sand or charcoal, or both combined, to remove organic impurities, which in various forms are more frequently the cause of dyspepsia, fever, cholera, diarrhoea, skin eruptions, and other diseases than many suppose.
>
> *The European in India*, Edmund Hull, 1878

Ice

So far so good, but as any seasoned traveller will tell you, abroad things are rarely as straight-forward and simple as they first appear. Assuming that you have now satisfied yourself beyond all reasonable doubt that the water you are drinking is fil-

Fig. 2

tered and purified, you would be forgiven for concluding that you were home and dry. How very wrong you would be.

Ice, unless known to be made from pure water, should never be put into drinks nor allowed to touch food.

Handbook of Travel, 1917

* * *

Iced drinks are deadly . . . The ice is usually full of microbes, all the more spiteful for their temporary imprisonment.

The Happy Traveller, Revd Frank Tatchell, 1923

It seems that even if water can be vouched for, ice (such an essential ingredient in the construction of any gin and tonic) may turn out to be of a far less salubrious pedigree. Indeed, this reminds me of a story told to me by my brother-in-law, Hugh Blewitt-Overall (for obscure historical reasons, pronounced 'Bung-Hall'), about a reception at the British Consulate in Naples in 1947, which points out the tricky nature of ice – even if you have been assured of its sound lineage. One of the guests at the party, a lady, was disturbed to discover a small object protruding from the side of one of the ice cubes in her drink. Closer inspection showed it to be a human tooth. Naturally there was a great furore, and the kitchen staff, waiters, etc. were all checked for tell-tale gaps in their dentition, but none that matched the rogue incisor was found. The Consul-General professed complete mystification, as he had a luxuriant penchant for having his ice shipped in every quarter, freshly hewn from the pure glaciers of Greenland. Fearing some sort of criminal act by the local Camorra, he naturally called in the *carabinieri*. However, when forensic tests were carried out, they revealed that the remains were approximately 2,000 years old, and it was concluded that the errant article must have originated from the grin of a long dead Inuit who had perished in the course of an ill-fated hunting expedition some 2 millennia earlier. The moral of this tale is that even those who imagine that they have done everything within their

power to avoid
unhealthy drinks
overseas should
never become too
complacent. Dropping
one's guard in this respect
may well result in plaque,
Eskimo gingivitis, or worse.

Fig. 3

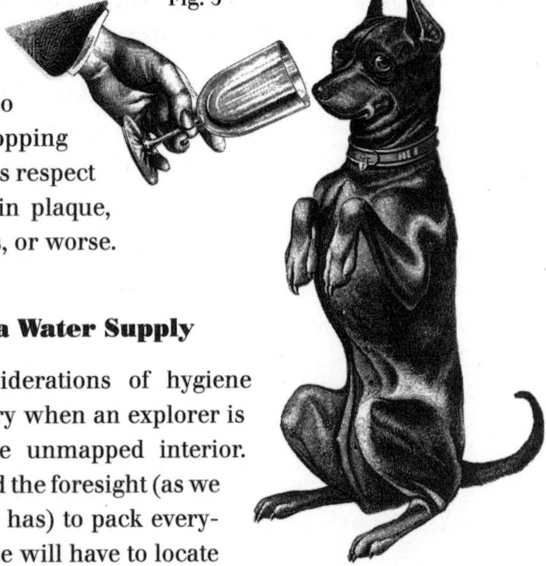

Finding a Water Supply

Of course, considerations of hygiene
become secondary when an explorer is
questing into the unmapped interior.
Unless he has had the foresight (as we
ardently hope he has) to pack everything he needs, he will have to locate
fresh water pretty sharpish if he is to avoid
perishing within a few brief sun-scorched days. It must be
assumed that even if he has forgotten to stow the mineral water,
he will at least have remembered to bring along a small pack of
hounds to help locate his nearest spring or pond.

> *Intelligence of Dogs and Cattle* – Dogs are particularly clever in
> finding water, and the fact of a dog looking refreshed, and it may be
> wet, has often drawn attention to a pond that would otherwise have
> been overlooked and passed by. Cattle are very uncertain in their
> intelligence. Sometimes oxen go for miles and miles across a country
> unknown to them, straight to a pond of water; at other times they are
> most obtuse: Dr Leichhardt, the Australian traveller, was quite aston-
> ished at their stupidity in this respect.
>
> *The Art of Travel*, Francis Galton, 1872

The wisdom of travelling with several dogs rather than merely
one or two will become apparent when it comes to water-testing.
The great luxury of being accompanied by eighteen of man's best

friends is that at least one or two may be regarded as expendable without precluding a spot of hunting later on in your travels.

> *Suspicion of Poison* – If the water of any pool at which you encamp is under suspicion of being poisoned, let one of your dogs drink before you do, and wait an hour to watch the effects of it upon him [Fig. 3].
>
> *The Art of Travel*, Francis Galton, 1872

In some regions even a canine with a first in advanced sniffing technique may find it impossible to locate a suitable water source, and the traveller who has miscalculated journey times or simply forgotten to pack adequate supplies of Buxton Spring Water will need to think quickly. Throwing oneself into a frightful panic and attempting to fashion a divining rod out of twigs or a metal coat hanger, or hopping about trying to cobble together an approximation of a rain dance, will only waste valuable time and energy. With a bit of resourcefulness, the fate of being found slumped beneath a tree as a wizened relic of leather and bone may possibly be averted (Fig. 4).

Fig. 4 *A few basic survival tactics can prevent a dangerous reduction in the level of vital body fluids*

Animal Fluids are resorted to in emergencies; such as the contents of the paunch of an animal that has been shot; its taste is like sweetwort. Mr Darwin writes of people who, catching turtles, drank the water that was found in their peri-cardia; it was pure and

57

sweet. Blood will stand in the stead of solid food, but it is of no avail in the stead of water, on the account of its saline qualities.

Vegetable Fluids – Many roots exist, from which both natives and animals obtain a sufficiency of sap and pulp, to take the place of water. The traveller should inquire of the natives, and otherwise acquaint himself with those peculiar to the country that he visits; such as the roots which the eland eats, the bitter water-melon, &c.

A Shower of Rain will yield a good supply. The clothes may be stripped off and spread out, and the rainwater sucked from them. A reversed umbrella will catch water; but the first drippings from it, or from clothes that have been long unwashed, as from a macintosh cloak, are intolerably nauseous and very unwholesome [Fig. 5].

The Art of Travel, Francis Galton, 1872

On one expedition, my five companions and I, having read the above advice, managed to survive for a period of three weeks solely on water sucked from the voluminous petticoats of the wife of one of our party. The absorbency of the underwear proved a godsend and we could have managed for a few weeks more if the lady in question had not started to resent having to stroll about in the rain whilst we were in the tent busying our-selves with map-reading, pipe smoking and back-gammon. Women are undoubtedly strange creatures, and we were

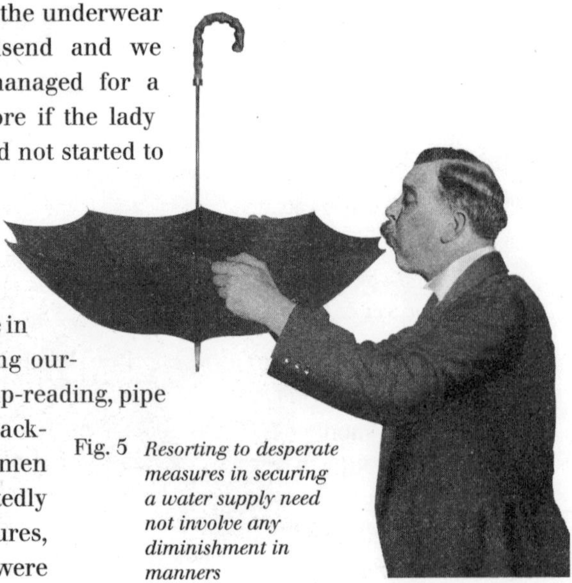

Fig. 5 *Resorting to desperate measures in securing a water supply need not involve any diminishment in manners*

forced to cut short our surveying work and return to a nearby village with our task unfinished as a consequence.

In Praise of Tea

The Englishman regards a constant supply of tea as his natural birthright, and any suggestion that he must abandon this habit whilst abroad should quite obviously be greeted with utter contempt. Besides, in order to produce a good cup of tea, water must be well boiled and this, combined with the natural antiseptic qualities of the beverage, is hugely advantageous to the traveller as a natural cleanser of the amoeba-infested puddle-water he encounters on his way.

There are few Victorian travel guides that fail to point out the efficacy of tea in the promotion of refreshment, health and comfort.

> The best restorative is tea, and as there are many parts of the Alps in which this luxury is hard to find, it is advisable to take a pound or half a pound from England.
>
> *Murray's Handbook for Travellers on the Continent*, 1836

* * *

> Tea, which may be purchased at the large cities, should not be forgotten in a Sicilian tour, for 'nothing', it has been truly observed, 'is productive of so much comfort, in proportion to the space it occupies, as tea.'
>
> *Murray's Handbook for Travellers in Sicily*, 1864

Mother Nature, despite some notable design classics such as the banana, the three-banded armadillo (Fig. 6) and the young

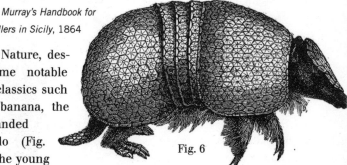

Fig. 6

Jean Shrimpton, has yet to come up with a form as compellingly beautiful and ergonomically sleek as the teapot. The rotundity of its body – pregnant with promise, the pleasing arabesque of the spout, and the jaunty effeminacy of the handle earn it a special place in the British psyche. Even the most unsentimental and aesthetically bereft of travellers would find it difficult to imagine a journey without one. Despite this emotional attachment, we must never lose sight of the fact that tea-making is essentially a chemical reaction and is prescribed by hard science. The traveller would do well to master the alchemy of the pot well in advance of departure.

The Theory of Tea-Making – I have made a number of experiments on the art of making good tea. We constantly hear that some people are good and others bad tea-makers; that it takes a long time to understand the behaviour of a new teapot, and so forth; and, lastly, that good tea cannot be made except with boiling water. Now, this latter assertion is assuredly untrue, because, if tea be actually boiled in water, an emetic and partly poisonous drink is the certain result. I had a tin lid made to my teapot, a short tube passed through the lid, and in the tube was a cork, through a hole in which a thermometer was fitted, that enabled me to learn the temperature of the water in the teapot, at each moment [Fig. 7]. Thus provided, I continued to make my tea as usual, and to note down what I

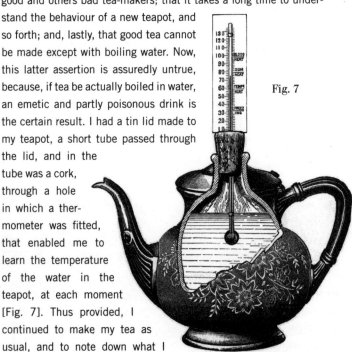

Fig. 7

observed. In the first place, after warming the teapot in the ordinary way, the fresh boiling water that was poured into it, sank invariably to under 200° Fahr. It was usually 180°, so great was the amount of heat abstracted by the teapot. I also found my teapot – it was a crockery one – allowed the water within it to cool down at the rate of about 2° per minute. When the pot was filled afresh, of course the temperature of its contents rose afresh, and by the addition of water two or three times repeated, I obtained a perfect mastery over the temperature of the pot, within reasonable limits. Now, after numerous days in which I made tea according to my usual method, but measuring strictly the quantity of leaves, and recording the times and the temperature, and noting the character of tea produced; then, taking as my type of excellence, tea that was full bodied, full tasted, and in no way bitter or flat, I found that this was only produced when water in the teapot had remained between 180° and 190° Fahr., and had stood eight minutes on the leaves. It was only necessary for me to add water once to the tea, to ensure this temperature. Bitterness was the certain result of greater heat or of longer standing, and flatness was the result of colder water. If the tea did not stand for so long a time as eight minutes, it was not ripe; it was not full bodied enough . . . There is no mystery in the teapot.

The Art of Travel, Francis Galton, 1872

Alcoholic Beverages

There is a theory that the entire British Empire was founded on chronic alcoholism, but as this thesis was first promulgated by the disgraced peer Sir Evelyn Strickland, who died of liver cirrhosis in 1898 at the Bethlehem Hospital, Lambeth, it is a point of view that is still very much in contention. However, the role of gin in the maintenance of British rule in India can surely not be doubted. Created as a seventeenth-century medicine for kidney disorders and now forever associated with Indian tonic water (invented in 1870 as palliative for malaria), the G&T has been found an invaluable panacea for thirst, malaria, tension, extremes of heat and cold, self-doubt, and slight feelings of glumness; and proves a remarkably effective pick-me-up for those performing such onerous tasks as Raj building and putting down local insurrections. It is therefore surprising that many of the guides I have consulted (even those written after 1870) neglect to mention the therapeutic quaffing of gin at all, and seem to favour the moderate usage of other drinks in its stead.

> While temperance in the use of spiritous liquor is earnestly recom-
> mended, it must, however, be allowed that there are occasions when
> the use of alcohol is imperative. In tropical regions, the depressing
> effects of the climate, except on robust constitutions, often show
> themselves in a general feeling of lassitude, attended with a feeble
> interknitting pulse and a sense of sinking in the heart. When such
> feelings are really experienced, as they often are after prolonged
> physical exertion, the use of pure spirit (whisky or brandy) in small
> quantities, copiously diluted, acts like a charm. With the single
> exception of best brands of champagne, the writer is unable to recom-
> mend, besides pure whisky and brandy, any other form of alcoholic
> beverage for use in the tropics. Beer and porter, especially the
> stronger kinds, provoke liver derangements, and claret of good quality
> can rarely be obtained by the traveller.
>
> *Hints to Travellers*, 1883

Mercifully, by the early twentieth century other writers were exhibiting a far more open-minded and adventurous attitude to sampling the local beverages:

> It is always best to take the local drinks of the country; e.g., Herva
> maté in Brazil; Apple-brandy in Kashmir; Cana in Ecuador; Lime-
> squash in the West Indies; Pulque-dolce in Mexico; Kwass or
> Kakatinski in Russia; Planter's Punch in Jamaica; or, if you are cold,
> a Pimento dram. In India and the Straits a good drink is a 'Virgin', a
> mixture of Vermouth and Gin. Gin is better for a white man in the
> tropics than whisky, and Rum is the wholesomest drink at sea. When

walking in Europe be careful not to drink white wine on an empty stomach. It fetters the legs and takes your wind away.

The Happy Traveller, Revd Frank Tatchell, 1923

But sadly, merely being prepared to sample locally-sourced tipples does not necessarily mean that the traveller will have the ability to appreciate some of the more willfully eccentric excesses of local custom.

The vin du pays grown in the interior of Greece is resinous, and scarcely drinkable at first by some foreigners, as it savours of vinegar and sealing wax. It is the custom to impregnate it with resin or turpentine, now as of old, whence, according to Plutarch, the Thyrsus of Bacchus was ornamented with a pine-cone. Colonel Leake has accurately described the ordinary country wine of Greece as 'a villainous compound of lime, resin, spirits of wine, and grapes, which, generally growing in a low and moist situation, furnish a juice without body or flavour'.

Fig. 8

Murray's Handbook for Travellers in Greece, 1884

Of course, there are thin demarcation lines between social drinking, self-medication, going on 'a bit of a jolly' and complete raging alcoholism. Whilst, in my opinion, a daily consumption of a couple of bottles of champagne, a few medicinal G&T's before meals, some restorative claret at lunch, tiffin and dinner, and a brace of large brandies as a nightcap can make the day pass pleasantly enough, drinking to excess should be carefully avoided.

A European, and especially an Englishman, should avoid countenancing the natives in the degrading and impoverishing habit of drinking alcoholic liquors. Much dirt has been thrown upon the good name of 'merry old England' by the worthless characters who have, as usual, been tossed forward by the wave of civilisation, which is fast spreading over Turkey. Instead of feeling that vice may be indulged in away from home, a man should be proud of his country, and prove it by sustaining her reputation and good name.

Murray's Handbook for Travellers in Constantinople, 1871

* * *

The practice of so many German travellers of taking small quantities of neat brandy or other spirit in Africa is most deleterious and if pursued for any length of time will inevitably prove fatal.

Hints to Travellers, Douglas W. Freshfield and Captain W.J. Wharton, 1889

CHAPTER THE FIFTH

*In Which the Traveller Seeks
Out Acceptable*

ACCOMMODATION

ACCOMMODATION

Once he is dressed, packed, fed and watered, a traveller's thoughts will, quite naturally, turn to procuring suitable shelter for the night. The form this takes will vary hugely from, at one extreme, the presidential suite at the Grand Hôtel des Bains on the Lido, to the other, a barely scooped-out hollow on a stony hillside in Abyssinia. Nothing will have more influence on a traveller's wellbeing than the accommodation he chooses or is obliged

Fig. 1

to opt for. With a good night's sleep under one's belt it is possible to put up with any amount of beastliness the following day, whilst to those deprived of adequate repose even the greatest of pleasures will feel dull and tarnished. But the modern adventurer prides himself on his ability to deal with any eventuality, and it goes without saying that he will greet all situations with the same imperturbable sang-froid. Thus, the difficulties presented by lodging with a truculent landlady in a guest-house in Blackpool and those posed by dwelling in a leaky tent in a crocodile-infested swamp in the upper Zambezi Delta will be regarded as much of a muchness. If anything, the former is likely to pose far more of a challenge: whilst it is permissible to dispatch a crocodile with a single bullet to the temple, it is currently forbidden by British law to deal with landladies in a similar fashion.

Hotels and Inns

Travelling around the British Isles as a preamble to a jaunt abroad, it is all too easy to grow accustomed to the availability of pleasant accommodation with obliging staff, efficient plumbing, a sewage system, glazed windows, a roof, walls, etc., but you will soon discover, within hours of leaving British shores, that not all the world does things as we do. As Dr Kitchiner observes, staying at one of our native hostelries can be every bit as fulfilling as visiting one's ennobled relatives for a weekend in the country, but even on these hallowed shores excellence is invariably the exception rather than the rule.

> The elegance and magnificence of some English inns and taverns, for instance, of the Albion in Aldersgate Street, are equal to those of many noblemen's houses; and the guests are made as comfortable, as if they were invited to occupy an apartment in the mansion of a man of fortune, with a request to accept the attendance of his servants, and of every thing that can contribute to their comfort and convenience: but the generality of taverns, in our opinion, are to be endured rather than enjoyed; and we do not envy the domestic felicity of those persons who prefer them to their own home.
>
> *The Traveller's Oracle*, Dr William Kitchiner, 1827

Most readers who have travelled to any extent will be depressingly familiar with the ennui that descends after the first couple of months staying in five-star luxury hotels, constantly being fussed over by flunkeys and consuming far too much rich food, and they will eventually be seized by an urge to seek out a far more 'authentic' experience.

A gentleman generally prides himself on an ability to fit in seamlessly with all manner of people, and will often feel drawn to the more boisterous taverns of a town in order to gain a few nuggets of insight into local custom. I can heartily recommend spending a lazy afternoon soaking up the *pastis*-fumed wisdom of a gnarled old peasant (Fig. 2); however, it is sensible to avoid actual physical contact with such types, as their teeth, nostrils and fingernails are known to harbour bacteria and toxins highly injurious to more refined constitutions.

The Reverend Tatchell, for one, recommends the 'mucking in with the locals' approach when selecting a room for the night:

Fig. 2 *Abroad, conversation need not necessarily be intellectual, or even intelligible, in order to be entertaining*

It should be your aim to live like the inhabitants, eat and drink as they do, smoke their tobacco, and read their newspapers. Above all put up at the inns to which they go, shunning the great hotels which are the same in all countries and where little of the intimate life of the people can be seen. Choose a hotel in the market-place of a town, and do not be easily dashed by the poor exterior of an inn which has been recommended to you by a native of the Country; the chances are that it is decent and well found inside.

If you have to register your profession in the hotel list, the word for private gentleman is rentier in French, possidente in Italian, and proprietario in Spanish. If this seems to you too lordly; simply write yourself down a student (étudiant, studente, estudiante). You may not be one in the literal sense, but, at any rate, you are a student of your fellow men.

The Happy Traveller, Revd Frank Tatchell, 1923

This is all very well and good, but unfortunately it does portray a rather rose-tinted image of what one might reasonably expect from foreign taverns, especially in some of the more far-flung edges of Europe. 'A student of one's fellow man' is one thing, but in some regions being a student of microbiology, parasitic entomology, waste management or mop utilisation might present themselves as far more sensible options.

The inns in the towns of the interior are with few exceptions filthy in the extreme, and destitute of everything which an Englishman regards as comfort . . . Brick floors unswept and covered with filth; walls foul with tobacco-juice, vermin and obscenities; sheets rarely clean, and often swarming with hungry occupants; towels that may have served a generation of muleteers; table-cloths with stains of a thousand meals; water scarce, and soap never to be seen; all appliances of the table of suspicious cleanliness, and cookery only to be stomached by those whose confidence equals their appetite – such are some of the features of the Sicilian wayside *locande*. To these may often be added a roof which fails to keep out the rain, windows that will not close, a door without fastening, and, to crown the whole, a landlord without conscience. In Sicilian country inns the traveller may expect less to eat than to

Fig. 3

be eaten. He may, however, sometimes avoid one cause of sleepless-ness by drawing his bed away from the wall.

Murray's Handbook for Travellers in Sicily, 1864

* * *

The Hungarian inns, that is, such as one meets with out of Pesth and other great towns, are, on the whole, the worst to be found in Europe. The apartments are dirty, the fare is indifferent, the sleeping uncomfort-able, and the whole affair quite opposed to what a person may reasonably expect, and generally experiences at the commonest roadside inns of other countries.

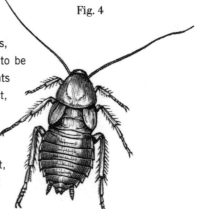

Fig. 4

Hardships in Travel Made Easy, 1864

The universal presence of vermin in foreign inns can afford an unexpected opportunity for sport. My old chum Reg Siskind tells me that he would never allow himself to get unduly riled by such inconveniences, as a very pleasant afternoon could be spent lying in bed picking off rats with an old service revolver. On one occasion, having exhausted the supply of rodents, he progressed to the greater challenge of targeting cockroaches as they climbed his curtains, but unfortunately this recreation was abruptly curtailed when one of his bullets ricocheted off the curtain-rail, narrowly missing a chamber maid who was airing some linen in the garden below.

Beware – after a few weeks' experimentation with lower-priced accommodation and a subsequent return to civilisation, the prospect of clean linen may have a tendency to turn a traveller's head. The surge of relief he experiences after a particularly protracted bout of squalor might easily topple him over the edge of what most Englishmen regard as decent behaviour and into the distinctly murky French realm of voluptuary.

> After a spell of rough accommodation and when you get to a good hotel, try the luxury of sleeping naked in fine sheets. On waking, stretch yourself well like a cat and get up quietly and slowly; to jump out of bed taxes the heart.
>
> *The Happy Traveller*, Revd Frank Tatchell, 1923

Bedrooms

It is time to give consideration to the level of sleep-worthiness of your room. Before judging your quarters too harshly, it is important to realise that a foreigner's standards of comfort and general cleanliness will very rarely, if ever, tally with your own. In the more lowly establishments, instead of complaining loudly that your room is barely fit for human habitation and confusing your host with concepts beyond his understanding, make light of adversity and regard the night ahead as an opportunity to test your resourcefulness.

> Procuring Beds when Travelling – One of the greatest difficulties which a traveller has to contend with is that of sleeping accommodation. Occupying, as in all probability he does, a comfortable bed at home, the positive discomfort which he experiences abroad is rendered comparatively the greater. In the first place, as travellers can never be sure that those who have slept in the beds before them were not affected with some contagious disease, whenever they can, they should carry their own sheets with them, or a light eider-down quilt and two dressed hart skins, the latter should be put upon the bed to prevent disagreeable contact, these should be covered by the traveller's own sheets.
>
> Clean sheets are rarely to be had at the lower class hotels and inns; the practice is to take them from the bed after a person has slept in them, sprinkle them with water, fold them down, and put

them in a press. When they are wanted again, they are, literally speaking, shown to the fire, and in a reeking state laid on the bed. The traveller is tired and sleepy, and only too glad to avail himself of the proffered rest, and without the slightest suspicion, he lies down on the bed, and probably arises the next morning with rheumatic pains, to which he may be a martyr for many months, or with the germs sown of a pulmonary complaint, which will never leave him as long as he lives.

Hardships in Travel Made Easy, 1864

* * *

Damp beds are oftenest found in inns that are least visited; they ought to be carefully avoided, for they not only produce dreadful disorders, but have often proved the death of the person who has had the misfortune to sleep in them . . . A Wash Leather Sheet, about 8 feet by 5, is not an unpleasant substitute for Linen.

The Traveller's Oracle, Dr William Kitchiner, 1827

If you do not feel equal to braving it out, it might be wise to avoid sleeping in the bed altogether. Sitting up all night in an armchair reading penny-shockers, smoking cheroots or playing the violin may pass the time tolerably enough, but a good night's rest is rarely achieved in this way. Instead, it might be better to throw all caution to the wind, ignore Nanny Bridlington's nursery rules from all those years ago, and opt for sleeping fully clothed.

Fig. 5

It will sometimes be prudent not to undress entirely; however, the neck-cloth, garters, girt, and every thing else which checks the circulation, must be loosened.

The Traveller's Oracle,
Dr William Kitchiner, 1827

Of course, wearing a thorn-proof tweed hunting costume in bed does involve a small risk of deep-vein thrombosis, whilst the likelihood of lung infections is reduced not a jot. With this in mind, I have spent a number of months finessing a plan with my tailor for the construction of a suitable sleeping suit designed to preclude the joint perils of damp, constriction, and infection (Fig. 6). I plan shortly to present it at a seminar on the Causes of Insomnia at the Royal Society of Master Bedmakers, but see no reason why I should not give readers a small preview here. The Immuno-Dri Jump Suit (patent pending) is a loose-fitting all-in-one

Fig. 6 *Too great emphasis cannot be placed on a decent night's sleep*

garment, with 100 per cent wool fleece detachable lining, a polyurethane outer shell and charcoal filter face-mask with shower-cap attachment. In my opinion, it is set to revolutionize an Englishman's ability to gain a good night's sleep abroad.

In the context of a decent night's repose, the following advice may be of use, but why the Reverend Mr Tatchell cannot invest in a decent pair of winceyette pyjamas is anyone's guess.

In noisy places plug the ears with cotton wool dipped in glycerine, and, when there is no blind to the window, open your umbrella and rest it on your body; should you be sleeping naked, and without bed-clothes, be sure to have a bit of sheet across the loins.

The Happy Traveller, Revd Frank Tatchell, 1923

However, there seem to be a marked inconsistency between the good vicar's evident aversion to noise and his penchant for a good aria.

> Like most men tramping along with the smell of the good brown earth in their nostrils, I sing or whistle down the road. But do you ever sing in bed? I do. My favourite aria is 'Why do the Nations' from the *Messiah*; and when I want to give myself a special treat, I muffle myself up in my bedclothes and hallo for all I am worth. A couple of minutes of this is just splendid. Then I compose myself for sleep, feeling at peace with all men.
>
> *The Happy Traveller*, Revd Frank Tatchell, 1923

Whether all men feel equally at peace with the Reverend Mr Tatchell after such a rendition is another thing entirely.

Paying the Bill

Like animals and children, foreigners can often be charming company, but as soon as you show any signs of weakness they are liable to walk all over you. So when it comes to the settling of bills it pays to keep your wits about you. In the most exclusive hotels, the payment of bills will never pose much of a problem. The service will be impeccable, and presenting the proprietor with a letter of introduction from the Archbishop of Canterbury coupled with a promissory note of settlement within the next three years will usually conclude your business.

But in moderately priced hotels it is advisable to take a different tack. Upon entering the foyer you should immediately contrive a small crisis in order to demonstrate that you are a man to be reckoned with. Instruct one of your staff to (accidentally) let loose your pet marmoset and allow it to rampage about the light-fittings for a few minutes before you yourself call it sternly back to sit on your shoulder (Fig. 7). Not only will this fix you firmly in the minds of the staff, but it will also mark you out as a figure of authority. Colonel Pearce's maxim of 'carelessly issuing a friendly wallop to the rump of a passing chambermaid with a well-aimed riding crop' is calculated to have much the same effect, but cannot be recommended unless you have the requisite 'front' to carry it off.

Once you have demonstrated that you are no pushover, you will be in a far better position in which to lay down some ground rules and make demands.

> Do not always take the first room which is offered to you and do not disdain to haggle over the bill. Foreigners despise a man who pays like a lamb. But do not see a cheat in every inn-keeper. Honesty is much commoner than you would suppose.
>
> *The Happy Traveller*, Revd Frank Tatchell, 1923

* * *

> In arranging for a room, the question of the daily bath should not be forgotten. This should not be regarded as a luxury, but as an absolute necessity . . . If possible the room should be found in a house containing a bath-room. But where this cannot be done, perhaps the best plan will be for the lodger to provide his own flat sponge-bath at an expense of from 8s. to 10s., and arrange with the landlady to fill and empty it daily. This service is not, in our opinion, one that should necessitate any increase in the charge for the room, or be regarded as other than an incident coming within the scope of the term 'attendance'.
>
> *Wit and Wisdom – How to Live on £1 A Week,* c.1890

Fig. 7

Despite one's best efforts, Mein Host will sometimes not be above some petty profiteering. It is at times like this that an Englishman's innate sense of justice comes to the fore. If your hotel is middling in range, and the proprietor has a reasonable grasp of English, it is far better to 'have things out' with him rather than let them fester.

> Never let your bill run longer than a week, and if you do not stay more than a night in an hotel, refuse to have the wax candles lighted, which are always in readiness on the toilet-table. It is gross extortion to charge 5 or 7½ groschen for candles that you do not burn half an inch. The best way of putting a stop to this practice would be by adopting the plan I myself once did – viz., taking them away with you. It was at one of the Heidelberg hotels. Scarcely more than the wick had been burned, but they figured in the bill for 7½ silbergroschen. On my remonstrating the waiter replied, 'We cannot use them again, if you remain here, sir, you will not be charged again till you have fresh ones.' 'Oh, then I pay for the whole candles, do I?' 'Yes, sir.' 'Very well,' I said, 'then kindly bring them down to me, and wrap them in a piece of paper. I'll take my property with me.' The idea grew upon me: I continued my collection, and kept myself in candles for a month afterwards.
>
> *Tourists' Annual*, 1868

As we have already seen, at the more lowly taverns along the road, attempts to explain that you are disinclined to settle up due to the fact that there was a dead goat in your bath (Fig. 8) or your bedroom lacked anything by way of a

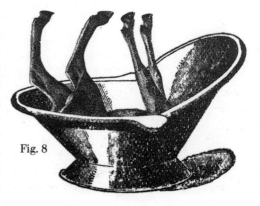

Fig. 8

ceiling may well be greeted by blank stares of incomprehension. It is unlikely that the proprietors of the more out-of-the-way hovels will speak (or admit to knowing) your mother-tongue. In this case, if fisticuffs are not your forte, you have sufficient funds and all you crave is the quiet life, then maybe you should opt for an acquiescent approach:

> I have always found remonstrance concerning the bill of no avail other than to add insolence to imposition – and I have constantly paid tavern bills without manifesting any objection, upon the principle of the man, who said that he made a point of never arguing with either a highwayman, or a barber; for one held a pistol to his head, and the other a razor to his throat.
>
> In the course of my last journey of more than four thousand miles, I never refused to pay for a single item in a bill of this description but once. I have submitted to sit in filth, to wait until I have been sick, and at last to get nothing eatable at an inn, at the same expense for which I had the day before been lodged handsomely, attended diligently, and served plentifully.
>
> *The Traveller's Oracle*, Dr William Kitchiner, 1827

Alarming Foreign Customs

Even when a *rapprochement* between your own standards and harsh reality has been reached, there is still the tricky area of local custom to contend with. What may seem normal behaviour to the locals will in all probability appear outlandish to you. We are all familiar with the unfortunate French predilection for the bidet and the bolster, and German beds too seem capable of raising the hackles of many an Englishman. The reader may also be interested in this early sighting of what has come to be known as the 'duvet':

> *German Inns* – A German bed is made only for one. It may be compared to an open box, often hardly wide enough to turn in, and rarely long enough for an Englishman of moderate stature to lie down in. The

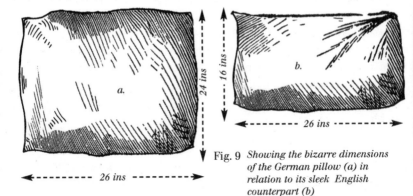

Fig. 9 *Showing the bizarre dimensions of the German pillow (a) in relation to its sleek English counterpart (b)*

pillows overreach nearly half-way down [Fig. 9], and form such an angle with the bed that it is scarcely possible to be at full-length, or assume any other than a half sitting posture. The place of blankets is sometimes supplied by a light, puffy, feather-bed, which in cold weather is liable to be kicked off, and to forsake, in his utmost need, the sleeper, who on awakening finds himself half frozen; should it remain in its position in the warm weather the opposite alternative is that of suffocation beneath it. Coleridge has recorded his abhorrence of the German beds, declaring that 'he would rather carry his blankets about him like a wild Indian, than submit to this abominable custom.

Hardships in Travel Made Easy, 1864

* * *

Germans have a horror of sleeping double. The beds, therefore, are usually much smaller than ours. The covering is also different, consisting of a light feather bed. In winter nothing is more comfortable than one of these beds; in summer they are too hot, and are replaced by quilts and blankets.

Tourists' Annual, 1868

I have often speculated whether I may have some German lineage myself, as I too have a horror of sleeping double with

Mrs Darkwood. But this may have more to do with her tendency to flail about in her sleep. She is not a small woman and she is liable to pack quite a punch if she catches you awkwardly. This is one of the reasons why I no longer allow her to accompany me on my travels. A traveller cannot always be choosy about his resting-place for the night, and trying to maintain an air of authority in front of the men is not helped if you appear sporting a black eye in the morning.

Other foreign customs can be equally curious:

> The keepers of coffee-houses and billiard-rooms (which are now very general) will always lodge a traveller, but he must expect no privacy here. He must live all day in public, and be content at night to have his mattress spread, with some twenty others belonging to the family and other guests, either on the floor or on a wooden divan which surrounds the room. When particular honour is to be shown to a guest, his bed is laid upon the billiard table: he never should decline this distinction, as he will thereby have a better chance of escape from vermin (Fig. 10). In small villages a traveller may consider himself fortunate if a peasant will afford him a night's lodging. The cottage of the peasant is a long narrow building, without any partition whatever, and admitting the rain abundantly. The apertures, however,

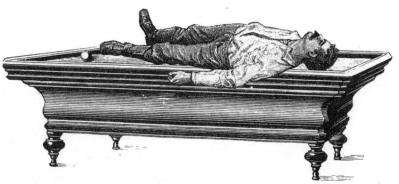

Fig. 10 *Ideas as to what amounts to 'comfort' will vary enormously depending on which country you happen to be visiting*

79

which allow its entrance are so far useful, that the smoke obtains egress through them.

Murray's Handbook for Travellers in Greece, 1884

* * *

Dutch Inns – As to the inns and public houses on the road, a person is sure to meet with clean linen, and soft beds, but their bedsteads, or rather cabins in the side of the wall, are placed so high that a man may break his neck, if he happens to fall out of them. Besides, a traveller must be content to be with half a dozen people, or more, in the same room, and be disturbed all night long by some body or other, if the churl of a landlord pleases to have it so.

The Grand Tour, Thomas Nugent, 1749

Contrivances such as bunk beds and other high mounted berths can be a particular danger to the older traveller. The youngster will nimbly spring up and down from one of these without a thought, but for a man in his sixties they can pose a very real danger. A case in point is the experience of an acquaintance of mine who during a steamer voyage was accustomed to lying upon the top bunk at night, enjoying a pipe and a book before sleep. Wearing only a nightgown, his habit was to leave his shoes and socks on to facilitate a final visit to the latrine. Unfortunately, attempting one such visit he slipped on dismounting his berth and found himself hanging upside-down by the ankle from a snagged sock suspender, in an outlandish pose reminiscent of Titian's *Flaying of Marsyas*. Being thoroughly overweight he was simply unable to right himself, and humiliation was added to injury as his nightgown inevitably succumbed to the forces of gravity and gathered in wreaths about his head. It was in this unseemly posture that he was found several hours of hoarse bellowing later, by a passing chambermaid. Mortified beyond belief, from there on he was too embarrassed to attend the Captain's table and remained sheepishly in his cabin for the rest of the journey.

CHAPTER THE SIXTH

Contemplating the Possible Necessity of

CAMPING AND SLEEPING ROUGH

CAMPING AND SLEEPING ROUGH

There are those whose natural flair for adventure would make them regard staying in a hotel or inn as the worst sort of namby-pambyism. In the pursuit of a more genuine experience of travel, they reject the cosy certain-

Fig. 1

ties of the *en suite* bathroom and sprung mattress in favour of the rugged life of the Tartar and the Bedouin, sleeping with only the merest piece of canvas separating them from the firmament (and sometimes no cover at all). The outdoor life is chiefly suited to those who need to travel far from the beaten path for expeditionary reasons, those whose tempera-ments dictate a close proximity to nature (robust types who enjoy tying knots, digging holes and defecating under starry skies), or those whose paltry finances will not stretch to a decent hotel.

The Romance of the Nomadic Life

Deep down, every man secretly fancies himself as a bit of a gypsy, a vagabond or a swashbuckler. 'If only,' he reasons to himself, 'I hadn't married so damnably young and opted for that safe job at the East Acton branch of the HSBC, things could have been so very different.' And indeed, who has not at one time or another found himself in front of the mirror, tea towel on head and curtain-ring dangling from ear, trying to emulate the derring-do of Douglas Fairbanks in *The Thief of Baghdad*? Even if family commitments militate against embracing the brigand's life full-time, a good few months of danger and hardship, riding and camping in the more inhospitable regions of the globe will at least allow you to catch a glimpse of it. When a traveller, saddle-sore, dust-covered and hungry, makes camp for the night all hardships are forgotten and poetry is born:

> If I might recall one hour, from this simple and nomadic existence, more delicious than the rest, it would be that of the evening bivouac when you choose your ground as fancy or caprice may decide – on a mountain-brow, or in a secluded vale, by a running brook, or in a sombre forest; where, become familiar with mother earth, you lay your-self down on her naked bosom. There you may establish sudden com-munity with her other children – the forester, the lowland ploughman, or the mountain shepherd; or call in, to share your evening repast, some weary traveller, whose name, race, and land of birth may be equally unknown, and who may, in the pleasing uncertainty but certain instruction of such intercourse, while the evening hour away with tales of the desert or stories of the capital, and may have visited, in this land of pilgrims, the streams of Cashmere, or the parched Sahara.
>
> Urquhart quoted in *Murray's Handbook for Travellers in Constantinople*, 1871

Another benefit of a nomadic existence far from England's shores is the satisfaction of knowing that all the familiar annoyances and petty distractions of life back home have been left far behind.

> Health is one of the secrets of the amazing charm which seems inher-ent to this mode of travelling, in spite of all the apparent hardships with which it is surrounded in the abstract. We pitch our tent wher-ever we please, and there we make our home – far from letters 'requir-ing an immediate answer,' and distant dining-outs, visits, ladies' maids, band-boxes, butlers, bores and button-holders.
>
> Richard Ford quoted in *Murray's Handbook for Travellers in Greece*, 1884

But where there is an enthusiast, there will always be a wet-blanket prepared to go that extra mile to cast a little gloom over proceedings.

> It is curious to see how many people there are who cannot enter into the spirit of the thing at all – people who tell you of inns and lodging in the places you want to visit, and descant on their dubious comfort and still more dubious cleanliness, never dreaming that you speak of living in a tent because you really prefer it to the more substantial brick and mortar of a stuffy bedroom in some little out of the way village public. It does not strike them what a grand thing it is to be in the open air from early morn till dewy eve. They wot nothing of the freedom of camp life, its absolute seclusion, and its marvellous healthiness. Some old gentleman who coddles himself over his study fire, and devotes all of his attention to a nice study of the cobwebs on a bottle of old port, will speak in utter contempt, if not downright anger, of 'young fools sleeping out in a wretched tent, with nothing but a rag of canvas between them and the outer air; when they might be stretching their legs between the cool sheets of a French bedstead in a decent four-walled house.' Truly here, if anywhere, the old proverb holds, 'What is one man's meat is another man's poison.' If you can't see any pleasure in the thing, our firm advice is don't try it. There are a good many discomforts and a good many rough experiences to be gone through, and nothing is more destructive of peace in the camp than a grumbler. He swears at the hardness of his bed, he swears at the smoke, he swears at the rain if it is wet, or at the sun if it is fine. There is never enough salt in the porridge for him, the stew is always burnt, and the bread always stale. He is sick of the whole concern in two days, and does his best to make everyone else of the same mind.
>
> *Gipsy Tents and How to Use Them*, G.R. Lowndes, 1890

Moaners generally anticipate that camping is bound to be a beastly affair, sleeping on lumpy ground besieged by insects, natives, rogue elephants and rain. But as we shall see from the following sections, whilst such eventualities cannot be ruled out, he must not also assume that 'cool sheets', and 'French bedsteads' are entirely off the menu either.

Home Comforts

There is a popular misconception, chiefly promulgated by scouty types, that camping is synonymous with travelling light and sleeping rough, but this, of course, is arrant nonsense. A hefty entourage of mules, horses, camels and native porters can make living in a tent a very pleasant experience indeed.

> The luxuries and elegances practicable in tent-life, are only limited by the means of transport. Julius Caesar, who was a great campaigner, carried parquets of wooden mosaic for his wooden floors! The articles that make the most show for their weight, are handsome rugs, and skins [Fig. 2], pillows; canteens of dinner and coffee services; and candles, with screens of glass, or other arrangements to prevent them from flickering. The art of luxurious tenting is better understood in Persia than in any other country, even than in India.
>
> *The Art of Travel*, Francis Galton, 1872

Fig. 2

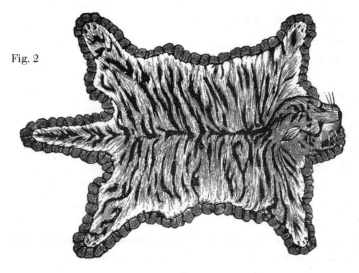

It is amazing how some ideas come full circle. I was extremely pleased to be told of an expeditionary suppliers, in Croydon, South London, by the name of Mr Ikea and Co., who currently offer an extensive range of 'laminate' flooring perfectly suited to a tent interior. Manufactured in handy interlocking pieces, it is a fine addition to kilims and a ground sheet, and a real boon to the style-conscious explorer. In addition to flooring they also specialise in cheap, light-weight 'flat pack' furniture cleverly designed for ease in strapping to the back of a camel. We experimented extensively with their merchandise during a recent journey through the Adrar region of Mauritania and found it to be most useful. Our porters had the Stäpp click-lock-action flooring down in a trice, and the Värde sink cabinet and corner shelf unit constructed shortly afterwards. The great advantage of this furniture is that on the last few days of your expedition you can chop it up and use it for firewood – as, in my opinion, though eminently suited to the rigours of travel, one plainly would not consider giving it house-room on one's return home to England.

Those of a more romantic bent may want to stick to more traditional appointments. Opting for the 'Full Tuareg' will not only give you licence to lounge on piled-up pillows all evening, smoking a pipe and wearing a fetching indigo turban, but will also have the power to infuse your mind with a whole wealth of beautiful thoughts.

Never can you better enjoy, still nowhere can you more easily dispense with, man's society than in your tent, after a long day's fatigue. It is a pleasure which words cannot tell to watch that portable home, everywhere the same, spreading around its magic circle, and rearing on high its gilded ball; as cord by cord is picketed down, it assumes its wonted forms, and then spreads wide its festooned porch, displaying within mosaic carpets and piled cushions. There the traveller reclined, after the labour of the day and the toil of the road – his ablutions first performed at the running stream and his *namaz* recited to gaze away the last gleam of twilight, in that absorbed repose which

is not vacancy, but a calm communing with nature, and a silent observation of men and things. Thus that pensive mood is fostered, and
that soberness of mind acquired, which, though not morose, is never
trivial and, though not profound, is natural and true.

Urquhart quoted in *Murray's Handbook for Travellers in*
Constantinople, 1871

Not all tent furnishings need be sumptuous and pleasing to the
eye (Fig. 3). Sometimes the prosaic and utilitarian reap practical
benefits far beyond the merely aesthetic.

> Two most necessary items of any African outfit, however small, are a
> portable table and a stout portable chair, and it would be better if the
> traveller took two or three chairs with him (as they are very light and
> portable) so as to be able to offer a seat to any native of importance
> who may visit his tent – an attention generally much appreciated.
>
> *Hints to Travellers*, Douglas W. Freshfield and Captain W.J. Wharton, 1889

Generally speaking I have found native chiefs a fine bunch of
fellows. Inevitably, one tends to rub the locals up the wrong way
a bit when building roads or railways through the middle of vil-
lages, ancestral burial grounds and such like, and the village
chieftain will naturally feel duty bound to kick up a bit of a stink
about it. More often than not, after inviting the head honcho for a
spot of afternoon tea or a few bracing Gin and Its at your camp, it

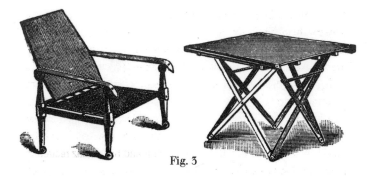

Fig. 3

will turn out that the fellow is a dyed-in-the-wool Cambridge man, and more than happy to spend a few hours regaling you with hilarious punting reminiscences, and scurrilous tittle-tattle about the porter of Corpus Christi and the Provost's wife. In such cases, a discreet cheque made out to his Swiss bank account is usually enough to oil the wheels of progress. If perchance, the headman is unfamiliar with Western customs, you may achieve the same results by proffering gift items such as pocket knives, beads, cheese graters etc., etc. For further guidance on this, see relevant section on Gifts, Tips, and Bribes.

Selection of a Tent

All in all, the selection of a suitable tent is a tedious business and as much a matter of personal preference as it is of practical utility. The best thing is to obtain a catalogue from a reputable supplier, peruse the illustrations over a brandy or two, send your man down to purchase your selection and ensure that you employ a bearer skilled in the handling of tent pegs, guy-ropes and other canvassy impedimenta. Alternatively, if you have both time and inclination you could sketch out an ideal tent on the back of a beer mat and have it run up by your local tent-maker to your own exact specifications (Fig. 4).

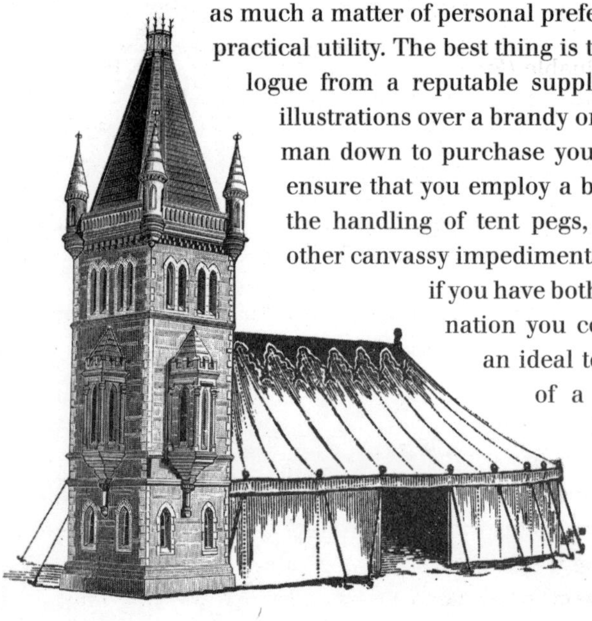

Here for your information is a brief 'Tents at a

Fig. 4 *A tent made to your own specifications can help avoid any problems of 'pokiness' that might be associated with living under canvas*

Fig. 5

Glance' (Fig. 5) gleaned mainly from Francis Galton's *The Art of Travel* and the Army and Navy *Catalogue* for 1907.

Fig. 6

In selecting a tent, Francis Galton's mathematical calculations of 'roominess' will prove invaluable (Fig. 6). As can be seen from the diagram, a properly designed tent should provide enough space for several mousta-chioed men to indulge in a jolly bout of stimulating social intercourse.

Beds

There is an unfortunate tendency amongst the young to regard the bedstead as an entirely disposable item. Each summer we see the despicable sight of thousands of youngsters swarming to outdoor music concerts around Britain bereft of even the most rudimentary camp furniture. Luckily for them, playing the idiot on home turf does not involve quite the same risk from dangerous fauna that a fellow is likely to face when abroad.

Bedsteads – A portable bedstead, with mosquito-curtains, is a very great luxury, raising the sleeper above the damp soil, and the attack of most creatures that creep on it; in tours where few luxuries can be carried, it is a very proper article of baggage. It is essential where white ants are numerous. A very luxurious bed is made on the principle of a tennis player's raquet; being a framework of wood, with strips of raw hide lashed across it from side to side, and from end to end. It is the 'angareb' of Upper Egypt.

The Art of Travel, Francis Galton, 1872

* * *

Some travellers take brass or iron beadsteads, which are a great protection against vermin.

Murray's Handbook for Travellers in Constantinople, 1871

A very useful technique I picked up during my Indian days was the habit of placing a soup bowl filled to the brim with salt water under each leg of my bed (Fig. 7). This was designed to deter ants, scorpions, cockroaches, etc., from scrambling up from the ground and making an utter nuisance of themselves. This worked very efficiently, but was of little avail with larger vermin such as rats. Of course, forming a moat between the bed and the floor was one thing, but it did nothing to lessen the attentions of fleas and bugs already in residence on the bed. As an experiment one evening I replaced the salt water with fresh ox-blood in the hope that it might lure my insect foes down and away from my person, but it was a hopeless failure. Instead of acting as bait for the fleas it merely attracted large swarms of flies, and it was impossible to sleep owing to the incessant buzzing. For more information on techniques of repelling vermin the reader should turn to the chapter on Health and Hygiene.

If straitened circumstances dictate drastically reducing your staff of porters to half a dozen, then the carrying of brass bedsteads and mattresses may become impracticable. Opt instead for a locally-sourced natural alternative, which can either be

Fig. 7

purchased from a trusted retailer or bagged by your own good self on a hunting expedition.

> Great use may be found in an oil cloth hammock, which may be hung from pole to pole, and is always of use to spread under the mattress when the ground is wet. It is easy, however, for a traveller to learn to dispense of a mattress and use a good fur instead, which can be procured in the country for a reasonable price. Should he be so fortunate as to procure a partially-tanned bear-skin, he will find it an excellent substitute for a mattress, which the bear's grease remaining in the hide will effectually keep off the vermin.
>
> Sir Charles Fellows quoted in *Murray's Handbook for Travellers in Constantinople*, 1871

The reader would be correct in assuming that there is something not quite British about the sleeping bag (Fig. 8), but if a traveller is really strapped for cash and bereft of staff it might be the only practicable alternative.

> *Bedding and Clothes* – it is all very well in theory to talk of rolling yourself up in a blanket and turning in. It sounds comfortable enough and easy enough, but a little time before dawn, when the night is at

Fig. 8 *Whilst being a desperately unstylish piece of equipment, the sleeping bag can, in a dire emergency, stave off the worst effects of exposure*

its coolest, you will probably wake up and find that the rolling process has hardly been as permanent as you could have wished. One end of the rug has disappeared, and the other is tucked away somewhere under your pillow, or in the corner of the tent. You pursue it for a bit in the darkness and then you begin to swear, and continue swearing until you bump up against the other fellow and make him swear too. You strike a light then, to prove that he has usurped half your bed (which he hasn't, of course), and get the rug straight at last and roll yourself up afresh. But your night's rest is spoilt, and your temper at breakfast the crankiest.

All this botheration and wretchedness, however, may be avoided by sewing your rugs up into a 'sack'. When once you are in it – there you are, they can't roll off and you can't roll out.

Silver and Co. make a very good sleeping bag, which they call the Pandora. The material is 'duffle', a sort of felt, very warm and soft.

Gipsy Tents and How to Use Them, G.R. Lowndes, 1890

Roughing It

If you find it necessary to make camp for the evening but have absent-mindedly neglected to bring a tent, quilt and pillow, it is theoretically possible to spend a night out in the open with very few deleterious effects to health, other than being swarmed over by insects, or slightly gnawed by small creatures of the night. A carefully prepared hollow will keep you adequately comfortable and out of harm's way till dawn.

> The cosiest place for camping is under a rock over-hanging a dry spot near a stream; the draughtiest is under a tree, but if I chance on a walnut tree I sleep beneath it as it is clear of midges and mosquitoes. These pests can also be kept at bay in the open by covering yourself with ferns. Your fire should be built in the shape of a half-moon with the points towards the wind. Build it quite small at first, using bark peelings of birch as tinder. Sleep on the lee side of it with your feet to the fire (the smoke will drive over your head), and have some spare wood by you to throw on during the night. If it is warm, use the beachcomber's pillow, your boots rolled in your coat. If it is chilly, your coat thrown over the head and shoulders is more protection than when kept on. To sleep snugly you must take off every perspired garment and wrap up well the coldest part of the body, from the waist to the knees. Scrape a big hole for your hipbone and use an old newspaper as a ground-sheet. Do not dread an occasional night in the open when you are benighted and have no camp. There are few beds more comfortable than a dry ditch in England in June.
>
> *The Happy Traveller*, Revd Frank Tatchell, 1923

* * *

Preparing the Ground for a Bed – Travellers should always root up the stones and sticks that might interfere with the smoothness of the place where they intend to sleep. This is a matter worth taking a great deal of pains about; the oldest campaigners are the most particular in making themselves comfortable at night. They should also scrape a hollow in the ground, of the shape shown in Fig. 9, before spreading their sleeping rugs. It is disagreeable enough to lie on a perfectly level surface, like that of a floor, but the acme of discomfort is to lie upon a convexity. Persons who have omitted to make a shapely lair for themselves, should at least scrape a hollow in the ground just where the hip bone would other- wise press.

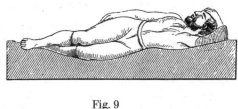

Fig. 9

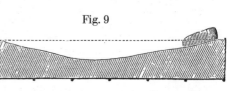

The annexed sketch [Fig. 9] represents a man sleeping in a natural attitude. It will be observed that he fits into a concavity of about 6 inches in greatest depth. (The scale on which he is drawn is 6 feet long and 1 foot high.)

The Art of Travel, Francis Galton, 1872

Such expedients are all very well and good if you have a reasonable certainty that the weather is going to remain clement, but after even a brief bout of drizzle, a scraped hollow has the tendency to become a muddy paddling pool and a dry ditch a picturesque babbling brook. Colonel Pearce was once carried off by a flash flood in this manner in Mozambique. After a slight over-indulgence in port the previous evening he had retired to a bed craftily constructed from rushes and palm leaves in a dry river bed, only to awake the next morning floating serenely in the middle of the Cabora Bassa reservoir.

When caught out by the elements and deprived of proper shelter it is sometimes advisable not to attempt to sleep at all, but to brave things out in the simple manner outlined below.

Improvised Tent – A simpler form of tent may be made at a moment's notice. If rain comes on, sit upright, joining the hands above the head as if you were about to dive, supporting the blanket on them, and allowing it to hang down on all sides that the rain may run off. If you have no blanket, you may still keep your gun, ammunition, or sketch-book dry by sitting on them [Fig. 10].

Shifts and Expedients of Camp Life, Lord and Baines, 1876

Hazards of Camping

The hazards of camping fall into three main categories, namely climate, wildlife and natives. Most of these will be dealt with in following chapters, but one or two are particularly pertinent to camp life and should be covered here.

Mosquito Nets and their substitutes – A mosquito-curtain may be taken for suspension over the bed, or place where you sit; but it is dangerous to read in them by candlelight, for they catch fire very easily.

Precautions against Thieves – Natives are apt to creep up to tents, and, putting their hands under the bottom of them, to steal whatever they can: a hedge of thorn-bushes is a protection against this kind of thieving.

Fig. 10

Preparations for a Storm – Before a storm, dig a ditch as deep as you can round the outside of the tent, to divert the coming sheet of surface water, and see that the ditch has a good outfall.

The Art of Travel, Francis Galton, 1872

In the event of an electrical storm it is wise to get one of your servants to stand with an open umbrella held aloft about a hundred yards from the tent in order to divert any potential lighting strike. Selection of a person to do this should be made on a strictly voluntary basis. Offering hefty danger money to a man known to have a particularly unhappy domestic life usually works a treat in this respect. Otherwise, if no volunteer is forthcoming, a cow or mule tethered to a post with an iron golf-club protruding vertically from the saddle-bag will do just as well. It is not advisable to use your favourite niblick for this purpose, as high voltages will have a tendency to warp such ironmongery, rendering it useless for your next visit to the golf course.

CHAPTER THE SEVENTH

On Mastering an Assortment of

EXPEDITIONARY SKILLS

EXPEDITIONARY SKILLS AND EXPEDIENTS

As we have seen, on any journey circumstances have a tendency to change almost by the minute. Eventualities and difficulties that might have sounded more like the fanciful imaginings of Mr Edgar Rice Burroughs from the comfort of your own home prior to departure, will become commonplace as soon as you step abroad. They will of course be of such a varied nature that it would be impossible to cover all configurations here, but by mentioning just a few it is hoped that the traveller will start to get an idea of what he is likely to come up against. With a modicum of lateral thinking and by pooling expertise and resourcefulness with other members of your party, a solution may be found to virtually any dilemma. An explorer's mind should thrive on problem-solving, but if all attempts at ingenuity fail then it is advisable to fall back on soliciting the help of locals by presenting them with gift items or large wads of cash. As we will see in the second half of this chapter, this method (especially if accompanied by a spot of unabashed pleading) can work just as well as rummaging around in one's brain for that spark of originality, if not better.

Making Fire

Back in England, if you were to leave home for the day sans Dunhill cigarette lighter, hat or hip flask, harrowing though it might be, the chances are you would survive the experience relatively unscathed. Abroad, however, forgetting to take your Patek

Philippe timepiece on a synchronised military manoeuvre or your old service revolver on a visit to a camp latrine can have potentially fatal consequences. And even if you do have the fore-sight to bring them with you, you had better make jolly sure that they are well-maintained and functional.

A case in point is the making of fire. Even if a traveller has the presence of mind to pack a box of matches, there is no guarantee that a spot of swamp-wading or a brisk breeze will not put paid to his incendiary aspirations.

> *Lucifers* – An inexperienced hand will waste an entire boxful of them, and yet will fail in lighting a fire in the open air, on a windy day . . . Consequently, in lighting a fire with lucifers, be careful to shield the match from wind, by throwing a cloak or saddle-cloth, or something else over the head whilst you operate . . . In a steady downfall of rain, you may light a match for a pipe under your horse's belly.
>
> *The Art of Travel*, Francis
> Galton, 1872

Fig. 1a

As your last Swan Vesta snaps in half or fizzles out in a disappointing puff of smoke, you might resort to traditional Boy Scout tactics such as scraping your knife against a handy flint (packed for precisely this purpose), and attempt to ignite some easily-combustible tinder, i.e., lichen, fine wood shavings, hair from the inner thighs of the capybara or lint retrieved from your own navel. However, this can be a time-consuming business

Fig. 1b

and a good alternative is to flag down a passing native and demand that he vigorously rub two sticks together.

> *Fire-sticks* – In every country without exception, where inquiry has been made, the method of obtaining fire by rubbing one stick against another, has been employed. In savage countries the method still remains in use; in nearly all civilised ones, it has been superseded within historic periods by flints and steels and like, and within this present generation by lucifer-matches. . . The process is as follows: One piece of stick is notched in the middle [Fig. 1b], and the notch slightly hollowed out; another is roundly pointed at one end. The fellow, being seated on the ground, holds down one end of the notched stick with each foot [Fig. 1a], and placing the point of the other stick into the notch, twirls it rapidly and forcibly between the palms of the hands . . . In a very few minutes red-hot powdery ashes commence to work up out of the notch, which falling on a small heap of lint is quickly blown into a flame.
>
> *The Art of Travel*, Francis Galton, 1872

From Fig. 1a it seems inexplicable to me why the fellow in question does not opt for lighting the fire using embers from the pipe he is smoking.

Once his hearth is ablaze, a traveller is unlikely to want to go through that flint, friction and flagging-down rigmarole all over again, and might opt to carry his fire with him on the next leg of his journey. If you are continuing your travels by river, for example, there is no need to assume that a boat is intrinsically different in principle from the snug bar at the Olde Cheshire Cheese, and with a bit of panache it can be made every bit as comfortable.

> *Fireplaces in Boats* – In boating excursions, daub a lump of clay on the bottom of the boat, beneath the fireplace – it will secure the timbers from fire [Fig. 2].
>
> *The Art of Travel*, Francis Galton, 1872

I have personally tried this technique in a rowing boat on the Serpentine in Hyde Park and, apart from the sadly predicable

Fig. 2

hysteria of the ticket staff at the boating house, found it eminently practicable.

Digging Wells and Carrying Water

Some methods of finding water were discussed in an earlier chapter, but simply discovering its source does not necessarily mean that you will be able to gain immediate access to it. Sometimes a traveller will find himself required to dig a well, having previously for reasons best known to himself, decided that a sturdy Wilkinson Sword spade, a bucket and wheelbarrow were not essential travel kit. At times like this sacrifices will have to be made and you may be forced to disfigure your Malacca cane by sharpening its tip into a handy digging implement. (The reader should note that a pointy stick can be equally useful in the planting of decorative shrubs, the digging of graves, etc.)

In default of spades, water is to be dug for with a sharp-pointed stick. Take it in both hands, and holding it upright like a dagger, stab and dig it in the ground, as in Fig. 3a; then clear out the loose earth with the hand, as in Fig. 3b. Continue thus working with the stick and hand alternately, and a hole as deep as the arm is easily made. In digging a large hole or well, the earth must be loosened in precisely the same manner, handed up to the surface and carried off by means of a bucket or bag, in default of a shovel and wheelbarrow.

Fig. 3a

The Art of Travel,
Francis Galton, 1872

Fig. 3b

Having excavated a sandy puddle of an alarmingly uric hue, the traveller will now no doubt wish to transport some of his find the three miles or so back to camp. A straggling line of, say, thirty porters each equipped with a picturesque earthenware pot is the ideal solution, but other clever contrivances can also be used.

In an emergency, water-flasks can be improvised from the raw or dry skins of animals, which should be greased down the back; or from the paunch (pericardium), the intestines, or the bladder. These should have a wooden skewer run in and out along one side of their mouths, by which they can be carried, and a lashing under the skewer to make all tight [Fig. 4].

. . . The Bushmen of South Africa make great use of ostrich shells as water-vessels. . . When a Dutchman or a Namaqua wants to carry a load of ostrich eggs to or from the watering-place, he takes off his trousers, ties up the ankles, puts the eggs in the legs, and carries off his load slung round his neck. Nay, I have seen a half-civilised

Hottentot carry water in his leather breeches, tied up and slung in the way I have just described, but without the intervention of ostrich eggs; the water squirted through

Fig. 4

the seams, but plenty remained after he had carried it to his destination, which was a couple of miles from the watering-place.

The Art of Travel, Francis Galton, 1872

On particularly hot days you may wish to try the above method whilst leaving your trousers on, although it has to be said, the cooling benefits gained by this variation are usually offset by a pronounced difficulty in walking, and there may be some debate when you get back to camp about the desirability of drinking water thus transported – no matter how gasping your colleagues are for a nice cup of tea.

Surmounting Petty Difficulties

Overcoming obstacles to the smooth progress of an expedition, such as crossing large rivers that according to your map should not be there or rescuing livestock and travel companions from abandoned mine shafts, are the bread and butter of the explorer's craft.

Make Shift rafts – Sir Samuel Baker says, when speaking of crossing the Atbara River, 'I had eight inflated skins attached to the bedstead, on which I lashed our large circular sponging bath, 3ft 8ins in diameter. This was perfectly safe for my wife, and dry for the baggage; the watertight iron box that contained the gunpowder was towed as a pinnace behind the raft. Four hippopotamus hunters harnessed themselves as tug steamers, and there were relays of swimmers. The raft answered well, and would support about 300lb, the sponging bath would carry 190lb.'

Shifts and Expedients of Camp Life, Lord and Baines, 1871

An essential piece of equipment for any expedition, I have found, is the Dalrymple All-Weather Typewriter/Harpsichord Cover. In inclement climatic conditions, such as monsoons or sand storms, trying to type out an epistle of love to your fiancée back home or a brief note to your tailor can be fraught with difficulty. The same holds if you are suddenly seized by the desire to tickle out a light fugue on a keyboard during a cloudburst. The 'Dalrymple'

Fig. 5   *Modern technology makes sure that the unnatural humidity of foreign climates never prevents an Englishman from indulging in hobbies in which clammy digits are seen as a drawback*

circumvents such problems and is also jolly handy for typing out secret missives away from the prying eyes of colleagues and natives (Fig. 5).

> Pulling a horse out of holes – The bight of a cord, or of some substitute for one, may be thrown over a horse's head, and he can be dragged out by a team of cattle with but very little danger to his neck.
>
> *The Art of Travel*, Francis Galton, 1872

I once had to drag Mrs Darkwood out of a patch of quicksand in a similar manner. Typically, she exhibited not an ounce of gratitude despite being saved from imminent death. As I pointed out, as long as she wore her high pearl collar for our next day's appointment with the Caliph of Zanzibar, nobody would even notice the rope burns about her throat, but no amount of reassurance seemed capable of consoling her.

At other times the skills required will be of a more perfunctory and domestic nature – such as ingenuity in the provision and the cooking of food.

> *Ant hills as Ovens* – Where there are no stones of which ovens may be built, and there are old white-ant hills, the natives commonly dig holes in the sides of the ant hills and use them for that purpose . . .
>
> *Ducks* – We hear of Hindoos who, taking advantage of the many gourds floating on their waters, put one of them on their heads, and wade in among wild ducks; they pull them down, one after another, by their legs, under water; wring their necks, and tie them to their girdle.
>
> *The Art of Travel*, Francis Galton, 1872

In the interests of scientific enquiry I have attempted to emulate this method, once again at the Serpentine, but on my first attempt the gourds, being an unusual sight on English ponds, failed to act as camouflage and simply frightened off any ducks I got close to. My second attempt was more successful. Selecting objects that would be less alarming to urban waterfowl, I adhered some Styrofoam kebab cartons to my head and kept my head below the surface using a snorkel made out of an old Coke bottle. The ducks and geese took my presence very much in their stride, and I returned home that evening a happy hunter, with four brace of mallard, a great crested grebe, one Canada goose and a heron hanging from my belt. (Though on reflection, if I were to repeat the experiment I think I would elect to be collected by car rather than catching the Underground home.)

Gifts, Tips and Bribes

The art of judging the appropriateness of gifts, tips and bribes, and what can realistically be expected in return, is an expeditionary skill that is usually mastered only with experience and practice, but it will be crucial to the success of any journey.

One of the sad aspects of modern life in the West is that everyone everywhere knows the market value of everything, and a traveller's largesse is generally regarded as a formality. Even further afield people seem to be getting more cynical and grasping with every passing year. The happy and innocent days when an explorer could purchase a chain of atolls in the South Pacific for three sacks of beads and a canteen of cutlery are sadly receding. Now, it's money, money, money all the way. But fortunately there are still a few remote patches of the globe left where the people are unspoilt, and stimulating barter can be entered into without recourse to the vulgarity of pounds, shillings and pence.

On deciding which gifts to present, it is tremendously important not to condescend to your hosts. Some 'new age' types may try to 'relate' to the natives by offering them shapeless hand-knitted items dyed with tree sap, or tragic daubs claiming to portray how we all live on 'one planet'. This is precisely the sort of artless tat that people in the third world are trying to get away from in the first place. A packet of Bic razors or a video of *Die Hard 2* is far more likely to win the hearts and minds of the locals than leftovers from a Camden Market craft stall. Other items that may come in useful are as follows:

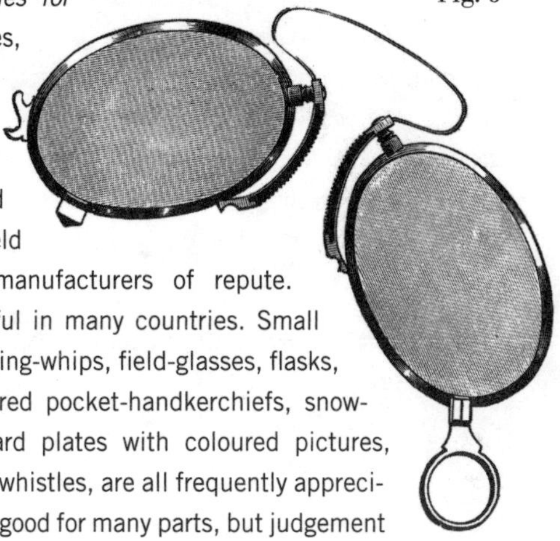

Presents and Articles for Barter – Clasp-knives, of all sorts, are esteemed. These are most advantageously obtained direct from Sheffield and Birmingham manufacturers of repute. Spectacles are useful in many countries. Small musical boxes, hunting-whips, field-glasses, flasks, tea, tobacco, coloured pocket-handkerchiefs, snow-spectacles, cardboard plates with coloured pictures, Waterbury watches, whistles, are all frequently appreciated. Beads are still good for many parts, but judgement is required in purchasing only those sorts that are in fashion. Information should be sought from previous travellers. A few simple conjuring tricks, and the knowledge of how to show them off, are often of the highest use to travellers in winning the esteem and respect of their temporary hosts.

Fig. 6

- *. . . 500 bead necklaces (amber, turquoise, &c.)*
- *250 silvered and gilt crosses, various patterns*
- *150 pairs of earrings and brooches*
- *300 eye protectors (green, blue, white, and neutral tint glasses)*
- *72 gilt and silver watch chains*
- *24 pairs of spectacles and eye-glasses (Fig. 6)*
- *18 tin dishes fitting one inside another*
- *25 tin plates*
- *36 tin spoons*
- *Silver toothpicks*
- *Keyless silver watch*
- *25 good pocket-knives (Fig. 7)*
- *6 corkscrews (Fig. 8)*

Fig. 7

- *Small tape-measures in brass cases*
- *Various plated goods*
- *12 circular looking-glasses*
- *12 mouse-traps*
  Hints to Travellers, Douglas W. Freshfield
  and Captain W.J. Wharton, 1889

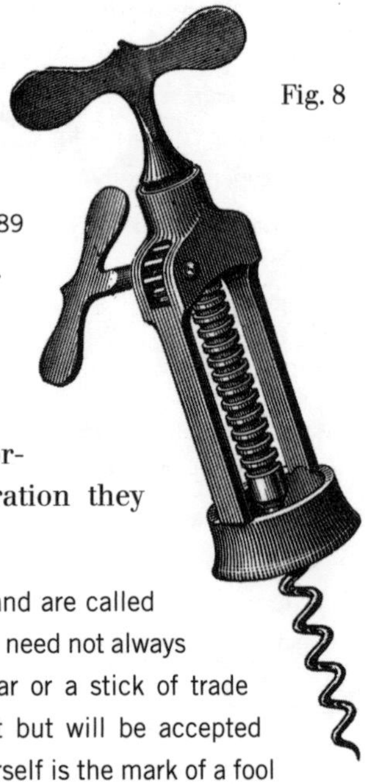

Fig. 8

In more cynical lands, nothing of great substance will be obtainable in exchange for cheese graters and Fuzzy Felt sets, but the traveller should never underestimate the impor-tance of the good will and cooperation they inspire.

Tips will be expected wherever you go and are called baksheesh or comshaw in the East. They need not always be given in money, a present of a cigar or a stick of trade tobacco will not only save your pocket but will be accepted without loss of self-respect. To stint yourself is the mark of a fool and to be niggardly in these little gifts is a mistake. I counteract my own tendency to meanness in these matters by unfailing liberality to children and old beggars . . . In Europe I take spare trout flies to give away to local anglers, and flower seeds for garden-lovers in other parts of the world.

The Happy Traveller, Revd Frank Tatchell, 1923

The closer one gets to home, the more the spectre of filthy lucre begins to loom over all transactions, but unless the traveller wishes to be at the receiving end of dreadful service and inso-lence wherever he goes he should not begrudge shelling out a few gratuities – hand over fist, and left, right and centre.

Be Liberal – The advantages of a reputation for generosity which a person easily acquires, and the many petty annoyances he entirely avoids, by the annual disbursement of five pounds' worth of shillings and half crowns, will produce him five times as much satisfaction as he can obtain by spending that sum in any other way – it does not depend so much upon a man's general expense, as it does upon his giving handsomely where it is proper to give at all – he who gives two shillings is called mean, while he who gives half a crown is considered generous; so that the difference in these two opposite characters depends on sixpence.

The Traveller's Oracle, Dr William Kitchiner, 1827

But be careful, becoming *too* reckless with one's largess, far from smoothing the way, can lead to ruin.

Affect not the character of a magnificent fool, whose greatness is manifest merely in the superior fault of squandering profusely. Some silly travellers spend so much in seeing other men's lands, that they are obliged, on their return, to sell their own.

The Traveller's Oracle, Dr William Kitchiner, 1827

There are countries where virtually nothing moves without the judicious application of bribery. An Englishman usually expects that his tweed suit and letters of introduction will speak for themselves in most situations, but in some quarters he is in for a rude awakening. Whilst endorsement from the Archbishop of Canterbury might work wonders in winning favour with up-market hotels and diplomats, most of the time you will find yourself dealing with sarcastic doormen, petty officials, traffic policemen, magistrates and other lowly beings. Unbelievably, your life membership of the Basingstoke Rotarian Association and your account at Fortnum and Mason will mean next to naught to such people, and a fiscal understanding will have to be reached instead.

On all occasions pay with both hands; every lock in Spain is to be picked with a silver key, and every difficulty smoothed by a properly administered bribe, and how small an additional percentage on the general expenditure of a tour through Spain is added by such trifling outlays. Never cross the Pyrenees to wage a guerrilla warfare about shillings and half-crowns.

A Handbook for Travellers in Spain, Richard Ford, 1847

Every city has its fair share of tramps and vagrants. These are people who have stumbled on the road of life and fallen on hard times. If they happen to approach you, you should always treat them with kindness and consideration. As you stroll along with the ambassador and his wife, or your pretty young fiancée, a gift of a few pennies will allow your friends to see that you are a man of compassion, and will also provide support for the vagrant to move forward in his life. If you are alone, a tremendous kick up the backside is usually adequate to propel him along the same trajectory.

The beggars in Italy are nearly as numerous and annoying as the fleas. The greater part of them are impostors, and should be dismissed with the words, '*Non c'è niente*,' which means, 'Nothing for you.' If anything is given, it should be the smallest possible coin. Fees should also be regulated by a moderate scale. English and American, as a rule, are too lavish. They demoralise the people, and make unpleasantness for other travellers by giving lire when half-lire will do, or fifty-centesime notes where they should give sous.

Cook's Tourist's Handbook for Northern Italy, 1875

CHAPTER THE EIGHTH

Suggesting a Suitable Choice of

COMPANIONS AND SERVANTS

COMPANIONS AND SERVANTS

A Warning Against Solitary Travel

Increasingly nowadays there is a trend for travellers to set out on journeys overseas totally alone. This is done for a variety of reasons: some adventurers maintain that travel companions are a hindrance to engaging with the local population and indigenous culture; others, such as transatlantic rowers and round-the-world yachtspersons, are compelled by overly-competitive natures to attempt some meaningless world record or other; yet others travel alone merely because they have not developed any capacity for making friends and to prove to themselves that they are not the freakish loner that everybody makes them out to be. Solo travel, in my opinion, is a highly over-rated sport, and chiefly

Fig. 1   *Deafness – not having the foggiest iota of what people are saying about you cannot be recommended as the best foundation for world travel*

the preserve of the utterly foolhardy and those with personal hygiene problems or personality disorders. There are also other traits that, far from suiting one to mono-peregrination, make it a highly hazardous undertaking:

> *Solitary Travellers* – Neither sleepy nor deaf men are fit to travel quite alone. It is remarkable how often the qualities of wakefulness and watchfulness stand every party in good stead [Fig. 1].
>
> *The Art of Travel*, Francis Galton, 1872

The current popularity of solo travel may well have its origins in the exploits of various television personalities who set out on voyages around the globe. The viewer gains the impression from the screen that the presenter is travelling alone when wading through the mangrove swamps of the Gulf of Fonseca or ingesting hallucinogens with the Babongo people of Gabon. What he fails to realise is that 95 per cent of such footage is filmed on a set built on a disused parking lot in Shepperton, and that on the rare occasions when presenters actually do leave British soil, they are accompanied by a vast entourage that includes cameramen, director, grip, sparks, gaffer, interpreters, bodyguards, personal valet, makeup artist, a luxury Winnebago and mobile catering unit. So let us hear no more nonsense about solo travel, and engage in the enterprise properly.

Friends and Relations

Travel is never easy, and the adventurer should not imagine that travelling with a large company of comrades and servants is necessarily the easy option. If anything, it makes the enterprise far more challenging.

The most natural course of action when selecting a travel companion is to choose somebody with whom you share a mutual interest. Whilst this does not necessarily rule out spouses, it does not necessarily rule them in, either. As we saw in the Introduction, leaving one's significant other at home can be instrumental in keeping a marriage healthy and happy – especially if one takes care to go on journeys on a very regular basis and ensure they are never shorter than eighteen months in duration.

> Even if you are married, sometimes travel alone. Identity of interests is by no means general in husband and wife, and there is no valid reason for a woman merging her taste in holidays in that of her husband. There is little question but that absence, gaily and mutually agreed upon, makes the heart grow fonder, and it is all to the good that we should recognise it.
>
> *The Happy Traveller*, Revd Frank Tatchell, 1923

The one advantage of travelling with a spouse is that you will be fully familiar with his or her foibles. Travelling abroad will merely entail a continuation of the low-level bickering that is the mainstay of married life – albeit in far more exotic surroundings (Fig. 2). The same cannot necessarily be said of friends or business colleagues. Acquaintances who might have seemed perfectly reasonable at the club or the office may well become a right-royal pain in the undercarriage the moment they leave England's shores. Great deliberation should therefore be exercised in their selection.

Fig. 2 *'Unhand me, you foolish woman.' Domestic bliss can no more be guaranteed whilst travelling than at home*

> Those who travel to foreign countries ought to be remarkably cautious in the choice of a companion for a long journey: if the person proposed have not exactly the same turn of mind,

the same interest to pursue; and if he be not a good-natured, active, and inquisitive man, he will be an intolerable burden.

The Traveller's Oracle,
Dr William Kitchiner,
1827

If you have any misgivings regarding the harmony of the group, it is better to put yourself in the position of senior man and delegate a few duties to your compan-

Fig. 3

Taking an instant dislike to your travel companions should never be allowed to hazard the success of an expedition

ions, just to keep them occupied. Whilst travelling with Colonel Pearce and Dr Reinhardt Flünkduster, the eminent shrew expert, I frequently had to instigate meaningless chores simply to divert them from a mutual animosity.

> If travelling in a party, it is always advisable to send one or two on ahead when approaching night quarters to make arrangements with the innkeeper. A party is always better attended to than a single person, and the road is always more cheerful. But the best number is always three. For if two quarrel there is always one to make it up or turn to. I have known two friends quarrel and travel for three days together sulking and not speaking to each other.
>
> *Tourists' Annual,* 1868

Forbearance is everything in travel, and it takes a big man to overlook the failings of others. Sometimes it is better to take the moral high ground and apologise needlessly to a self-evident fool in order to maintain harmony in the camp – whilst making a mental note to lace his cup of tea with rat guano and laxatives at the very next opportunity.

> *Good Temper* – Tedious journeys are apt to make companions irritable one to another; but under hardened circumstances, a traveller does his duty best who doubles his kindliness of manner to those about him, and takes harsh words gently, and without retort. He should make it a point of duty to do so. It is at those times very superfluous to show too much punctiliousness about keeping up one's dignity, and so forth; since the difficulty lies not in taking up quarrels, but in avoiding them.
>
> *The Art of Travel*, Francis Galton, 1872

At other times, proof of one's manhood can be achieved by more traditional methods:

> Everything during a journey beyond the limits of civilisation depends upon the good feeling and harmony among the party, and nothing short of unavoidable necessity should be suffered to interfere with this.

Fig. 4

> In one case related to us, one of the travellers had been called a coward by his comrade because he failed to fire at a lion at the expected moment. His reply was, 'We will not quarrel over it now; but we separate at the first opportunity, and meantime I may find a chance to prove that I have not deserved your reproach.' One day he who had been thus stigmatised remained at home; and, when his comrade returned, said to him – 'I thought I should be able to show that your words were undeserved: a lion has attacked the camp.' 'Where is he?' asked the other. 'Lift up the covering, and you will see him here,' was the reply. There was but one wound – it was in the forehead – and from so short a distance had the death shot been discharged that the flash of the gun had singed the hair around the orifice it had made. The accuser apologised for his hasty words; but the breach was never healed, and the separation took place soon after [Fig. 4].
>
> *Shifts and Expedients of Camp Life*, Lord and Baines, 1876

Although it may involve a few trifling quarrels, journeying in a group does have its compensations. Well-selected travel companions will always be there to help out in any situation. They are particularly useful in sucking the poison out of embarrassingly placed snakebites or acting as an audience for your lengthy campfire reminiscences. On one memorable occasion Dr Flünkduster acted selflessly (albeit unwittingly) as a diversionary decoy from the unwanted attentions of a particularly angry tiger. Pearce had already taken a pot-shot at the beast, singeing its left ear, but after that his rifle had jammed. Face to face with his foe, he fortunately had the presence of mind to chuck a large stone at Flünkduster, who was bending down to examine a botanical specimen at the time. The rock made the eminent shrew expert yelp loudly, thus diverting the big cat's attention from us to him, and allowing us to escape unscathed. Despite his heroism and our unflinching praise, Flünkduster was inexplicably touchy when he eventually scrambled down from the tree and joined us for dinner some five hours later.

Animal Companions

Anyone who has been on a lengthy expedition will be familiar with the menagerie of marmosets, gibbons, bird-eating spiders, anacondas, etc. that one inevitably accumulates as pets along the way. Strictly speaking these cannot be classified as companions in a real sense, but more as temporary hitchhikers. The same thing goes for the horse and other beasts of burden, who are far too busy with practical matters to provide actual comradeship. No, the only animal that can really be regarded as a proper travel companion is a dog. In packs, dogs instantly revert to being beasts, but individually they can be charming company. They are loyal, affectionate and utterly devoted to their master's welfare. What is more, they can always be relied upon, if the going gets tough, to make the greatest sacrifice a friend has to offer, and volunteer themselves as the principal ingredient of a delicious Korean barbecue for twelve.

Care should be taken when transporting a dog by carriage. You may well regard him as your best friend, but it does not necessarily follow that he will rub along as spiffingly with other species. A few rudimentary precautions should be taken to avoid guilt by association.

> A dog may be carried in a net or bag slung under the carriole, upon the Italian plan. It is always the safest way to carry a dog in that manner in case of his being attacked by a wolf, for with that animal a dog is an irresistible temptation. Pigs and cattle will also frequently attack a strange dog very fiercely, perhaps mistaking him for a wolf.
>
> *Murray's Handbook for Travellers in Denmark, Norway,*
> *Sweden, and Iceland*, 1858

If you stop for a while at any location abroad, you would do well to remember that anywhere where the sun shines more than in England – i.e. more than six days over the average summer – there is bound to be an impressive catalogue of incurable diseases to catch. And what applies to humans can also apply to dogs.

People in England seem to labour under the impression that dogs, in India, have a tendency invariably to go mad, and frequently, in consequence, beg their friends not to keep such dangerous pets. This idea is partly a reasonable one, for of course the heat of the climate is inimical to English dogs, as it is to Englishmen; and the former do, without doubt, sometimes go mad when neglected; though hardly ever, if well cared for by kindly and intelligent owners. Masters frequently leave home for a month or two, to brace and refresh themselves on the hills, without choosing to remember, that Dash or Tan is as great an exotic as themselves; and that he too would be all the better for a run along the hill sides, and a ramble on the mountain tops. Indeed, he requires much to compensate him for the annoyances he suffers on the plains, what with the heat, the flies, the fleas, and that special enemy of dogs, the tic, or dog poochey.

. . . Not long ago, a terrible case, in which the life of a young English doctor was sacrificed, occurred in Kurnool. An officer from that station went away to the hills, leaving his dog at home in charge of the servants. After a time the animal became sullen, refused his food, and snapped at those who came near him. The servant, thereupon, took him to the doctor of the regiment for inspection. The latter, with a lamentable rashness, took the dog and attempted to open his

Fig. 5

mouth, but, while doing so, received a severe bite, and shortly after-wards died of hydrophobia.

The European in India, Edmund Hull, 1878

To her eternal embarrassment, on her last trip with me to the Punjab Mrs Darkwood picked up a fearful array of dog poocheys after a picnic in the Shalimar Gardens in Lahore. It took a good three hours with hot water, tweezers and Vaseline to extricate the little blighters, and she was unable to ride side-saddle for two weeks after.

English Servants

After deciding on suitable companions, the traveller must next move on to the problematic area of selecting appropriate staff. On a journey of five months or more I would simply refuse to budge without a basic complement of English servants – say, my trusty batman, Stour-bridge; chef, sous-chef and pastry cook; and a special-ist bag-boy for carrying precious items and delic-ate scientific instruments. (Nanny Bridlington, despite her homely wisdom and pie-making abilities, is invariably left at home, as abroad is no place for a woman well into her eighties and her dot-age.) Generally speaking, all other staff can safely be hired abroad.

Fig. 6 *A young proletarian receives instruction on the non-lopsided conveyance of heavy objects*

The specialist bag-boy is of particular importance, as foreign porters should never be trusted to carry luggage of extreme value or fragility. He should be trained prior to departure according to the Greenwell-Bruce Method, a system of training the lower orders to carry heavy weights with poise, equilibrium and reliability (Fig. 6). (For further information, refer to *Practical Management of Menials* by Maurice Greenwell and Auberon Bruce, London 1909.)

A batman or personal valet should also be scrutinised and questioned as to his qualifications, character and adaptability:

> A traveller exposes himself to many inconveniences if he cannot depend upon the fidelity and sobriety of his servant, and his aversion to illicit and dangerous amusements – his character cannot be too closely scrutinised before an agreement takes place.
>
> A servant selected to accompany a gentleman on his travels, should be conversant with the French language, write legibly, and be able to copy with correctness and celerity whatever is laid before him; it will be extremely convenient that he can occasionally officiate as cook, or horse and carriage keeper.
>
> *The Traveller's Oracle*, Dr William Kitchiner, 1827

On the whole, though, domestic staff seldom measure up to the exacting standards prescribed by their masters. Abroad, staff often reveal themselves as drippy creatures bereft of moral fibre.

> English servants should as much as possible be dispensed with in Levantine travel. They are usually little disposed to adapt themselves to strange customs, have no facility in acquiring foreign languages, and are more annoyed by hardships and rough living than their masters. Indeed, it is not merely troublesome and expensive, but entirely useless in a journey through Greece, to take any attendants in addition to the travelling servants of the country. Those who may have them in their service would do advisably to leave them at Corfu or Athens during the journey.
>
> *Murray's Handbook for Travellers in Greece*, 1884

* * *

No lady who values her peace on the journey, or desires any freedom of mind or movement, will take a maid. What can a poor English girl do who must dispense with home-comforts, and endure hardships that she never dreamed of, without the intellectual enjoy-ments which to her mistress compensate (if they do com-pensate) for the inconveniences of Eastern travel? If her mistress has any foresight, or any com-passion, she will leave her at home. If not, she must make up her mind to ill-humour or tears, to the spectacle of wrath or despondency, all the way. If she will have her maid, let her, at all events, have the girl taught to ride – and to ride well; or she may have much to answer for.

Fig. 7

Eastern Life, Harriet Martineau, 1848

Of all the staff I have ever employed, Stourbridge alone exhibits the steadfastness and pluck absolutely indispensable in a right-hand man. He is the mainspring of my expeditionary staff and simply worth his weight in gold – as one episode amply demon-strates: I was returning to camp one afternoon when I espied from a distance Stourbridge and Mrs Darkwood acting rather strangely. Stourbridge was kneeling at my spouse's feet and looking up at her. As I drew closer, Stourbridge pounced, pushing my good lady wife violently off her feet and frantically rummag-ing about in her crinolines. By the time I got to them, both were quite out of breath. They looked startled as I ran up and Mrs Darkwood stammeringly explained that my trusty batman had seen a scorpion crawling up her skirts and had been trying to find the blighter before it got up to any mischief. Few servants in the face of such mortal danger would have acted with such selfless bravery. Mrs Darkood had evidently been in a state of great nervous distress, as her extreme terror had exhibited itself in a peculiar way. Throughout the drama, instead of screaming, she had merely emitted a series of shrill girlish giggles strangely incongruent with the life-threatening peril in which she had found herself.

Foreign Servants

The main bulk of servants required for an expedition can be hired locally. These will vary according to personal taste but, generally speaking, engage enough staff to cover these various roles: horse-boy, postilion, dragoman, personal valet, interpreter, medic, laundress, masseur, cutlery-boy, keeper of sports accoutrements, croupier, etc., etc. It is also wise to hire a taciturn muscle-bound henchman (usually called something like Tonton or Chooktah) who stands about looking utterly menacing (Fig. 8). His role is unspecified, but times are bound to arise when you'll be jolly pleased to have such a staff member around.

The selection of local servants can be a bit of a minefield, but there are certain considerations to take into account:

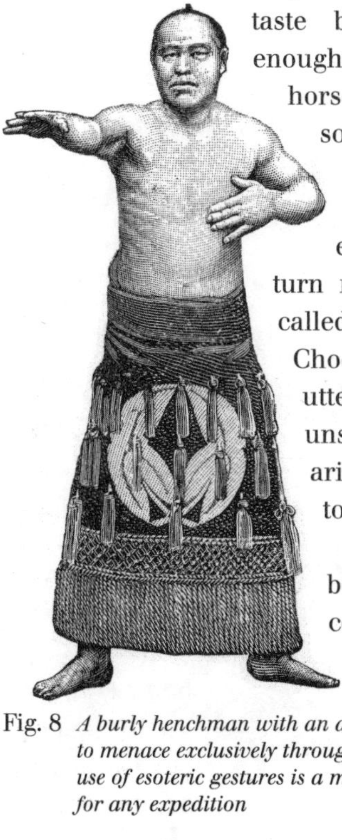

Fig. 8 *A burly henchman with an ability to menace exclusively through the use of esoteric gestures is a must for any expedition*

A good servant, though not necessary, is a great comfort in the East and is not an expensive luxury; being carried for nothing on the steamers and for a mere trifle on the trains. In India choose a Madrassi because, although probably a rascal, he does not trouble about caste and can speak (atrociously) nearly all the dialects. But do not let him become too familiar. He must not enter your presence shod or bareheaded. Remember that a white man is a 'big chief' in the Tropics and keep your dignity, and, especially, never shake hands with a native.

Beyond India, John Chinaman is the servant to have, and a Chinese woman, who has been trained, makes the best nurse for a sick or wounded man. Engage no guide; if you do, he will spend most of the time leading you round to show you off to his various acquaintances.

The Happy Traveller, Revd Frank Tatchell, 1923

* * *

Servants, a necessary evil anywhere, are especially so in the East. The traveller may indeed, if he only intends visiting Alexandria and Cairo, and the line of the Suez Canal, do without them, or at any rate he need only hire an occasional *valet de place*, at from 5*s* to 8*s* a day, according to the service rendered. But if he intends to travel about, he must provide himself with one or more; and should he know nothing of the country or the language, a dragoman (*terjumán*) will be indispensable. The dragoman, literally an interpreter, will take all trouble off his hands, and for a fixed sum defray all the expenses of travelling, food, lodging and servants, &c.

All who can should, before leaving England, get a dragoman recommended to them by friends who have had experience of him: it will save them a great

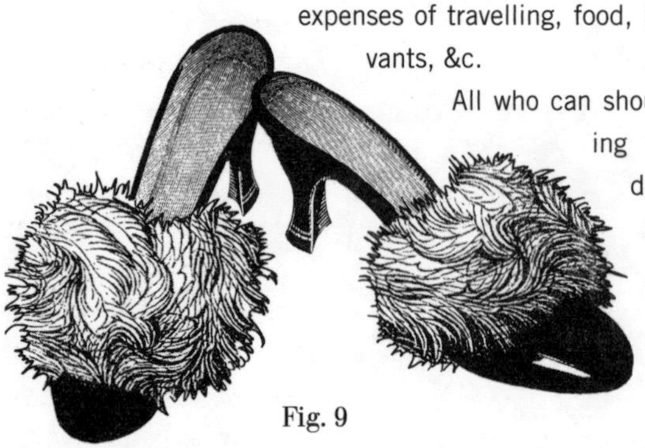

Fig. 9

deal of trouble, and they will feel more sure of the sort of man they have to deal with.

Murray's Handbook for Travellers in Egypt, 1880

Any agreement you enter into with local servants is likely to be tested to the limits by more unscrupulous employees. If kind words and firmness fail, refer recalcitrant underlings to the small print of their contract – in Subsection 2a, regarding your 'right to resolve any disagreement with a bloody good thrashing with a knobbly stick'.

A favourite imposition of the *agoyates* (horse-boys) is to extort money from the traveller during the journey, on the pretext that the feeding of the horses was not included in the contract. Should the traveller refuse, they resort to the coercion of starving the animals, or turning them into corn-fields, when the traveller is made liable for the damage done . . . Unless the traveller is firm, and early shows himself prepared to look after his own interests, such contretemps will occur even with a good dragoman.

Murray's Handbook for Travellers in Greece, 1884

In engaging staff, make sure that your needs are clear and your requests are well understood. Some years ago, after staying for a week in Chiang Mai on a journey to Thailand, my colleagues and I planned a trip into the interior the following day over rough terrain. We therefore needed to hire a muleteer and some reliable pack animals to carry our supplies. That evening I asked the proprietor of the hotel if he could arrange 'a fine pair of mules and a boy capable of giving satisfaction to an English gentleman' for the following morning. Wires must have got well-and-truly crossed somewhere along the way, as when a knock came at my door at seven the next morning, in place of the burly farmhand I had envisaged stood a wiry effeminate-looking fellow wearing mascara and lip-gloss, and clasping a pair of satin and ostrich-feather lady's slippers in his hands (Fig. 9). I could only dissuade him from gaining ingress by referring him to Subsection 2a within an inch of his life.

Other than those entrusted to the specialist bag-boy, all supplies will be carried by pack animals, natives and porters. These might be regarded as the least skilled end of your staff spectrum, and therefore should be treated with added firmness.

> In all dealings with camp-servants and natives be first of all patient, next just and firm, dealing praise and blame alike sparingly, but heartily. Never lose your temper – except on purpose, and avoid banter.
>
> *Hints to Travellers*, Douglas W. Freshfield and Captain W.J. Wharton, 1889

All in all, one's entourage of companions and staff should be regarded as a big jolly extended family: some will be awkward and unbiddable; others prone to fits of melancholia; yet others easy-going and accommodating; whilst junior members may be 'into' outlandish music, theft and arson. But travel companions do have one great advantage over family members – after a protracted period of journeying they can be totally jettisoned and, if you prefer, never ever seen again.

CHAPTER THE NINTH

*In which we Compare and
Contrast Various*

MODES OF
CONVEYANCE

MODES OF CONVEYANCE

When planning a holiday, an expedition or a tour of the globe, choosing an appropriate mode of conveyance is an enormously important consideration. To cover the subject adequately might easily take a hundred times the space available to us here, but it is hoped that if we merely touch upon a few salient aspects of our more common forms of transport the reader will be fired up with a frenzied urge to research the subject more widely.

Fig. 1

On Foot

When yielding to the instinct to roam, what could be more natural than for a traveller to set out on his own two feet? Shanks's pony may be slow, plebeian and wholly unsophisticated, but it certainly has the advantage of getting one from A to B with the minimum amount of fuss and the minimum amount of expenditure. Walking also affords opportunities to observe indigenous peoples at close hand, to scrutinise details of passing scenes and landscapes, to get to grips with one's host's culture, and to chortle away in wry amusement at the ghastly absurdity of it all. It is also eminently good for one's health:

> There is no exercise equal to walking in the open air; it invigorates
> the body and exhilarates the mind: – after a smart walk for an hour
> or more, I return home in much higher spirits, than if I had sat still
> and drank a tumbler of wine . . . One of the best moderators of mor-
> bidly acute feeling, is exercise continued almost to fatigue. A man
> suffering under a fit of the vapours, after half an hour's brisk ambu-
> lation, will often find that he has walked it off, and that the action of
> the body has exonerated the mind.
>
> *The Traveller's Oracle*, Dr William Kitchiner, 1827

Health considerations apart, a man of fashion might harbour
misgivings about the sartorial implications of walking. Strolling
about town will pose no serious problem, but in embarking on a
walk in the country he will be uncomfortably aware that he is
entering the dominion of the chunky-knit rambling brigade.
Images of hairy-eared pensioners and gawky misfits charging up
mountainsides with brown knees, lederhosen, cagoules and
carbon-fibre ski sticks might well dampen his enthusiasm. But
rest assured – there is no mystery to cutting a dash on the mountainside. At all times wear tweed and brogues (Fig. 1), and those
of a more flamboyant bent can always embellish this outfit with
the addition of romantic items of peasant costume.

> A very admirable article in a traveller's wardrobe is a Blouse (*Kittel* in
> German), somewhat resembling a ploughman's smock-frock in
> England, but by no means confined to the lower orders abroad, as it
> is a common travelling costume of nobles, gentles, and peasants. It
> may be worn either over the usual dress, to keep it clean and free
> from dust, or it may be substituted for the coat in hot weather. In
> either case it is very serviceable. This kind of garment may be pur-
> chased ready-made in any German town. The best colour is brown;
> blue is usually worn by agricultural labourers only.
>
> *Murray's Handbook for Travellers on the Continent*, 1836

A walker not used to spending long days on the open road may
eventually succumb to abominable chafing and advanced 'hide

tweak'. In the absence of a qualified physician he will be thrown back onto his own resources, and it is essential that he have a few valuable home remedies up his sleeve to use in the case of emergencies.

> To prevent the feet from blistering, it is a good plan to soap the inside of the stocking before setting out, making a thick lather all over it. A raw egg broken into a boot, before putting it on, greatly softens the leather: of course the boots should be well greased when hard walking is anticipated.
>
> *The Art of Travel*, Francis Galton, 1872

* * *

> If your feet become tender, rub them with brandy, and pour half a glass of *Schnapps* (brandy) into your shoes before putting them on. If you should have a blister, draw a needle and worsted carefully through it before going to bed, and anoint with a little deer fat (*Hirsch Talg*) which you can get at any apothecary's for a couple of half-pence, and will find invaluable. Don't drink too much water.
>
> *The Tourists' Annual*, 1868

The novelty of stomping about on foot is bound to wear a bit thin the moment the pedestrian becomes aware of the huge array of energy-saving contraptions that are on offer to those able to afford them. Health is all very well and good, but shiny paintwork, windscreens, wheels, bells, chrome and throbbing motors are apt to turn a man's head. Save time and energy, and get someone or something else to do the slog for you.

Sedan Chairs and Palanquins

Before setting off at a gallop, let us first direct our attention towards one of the oldest and simplest means of transport – the sedan chair. Even such a rudimentary device comes in a startling array of forms, but all are embodiments of the same basic contractual agreement – i.e., 'I simply can't be bothered using my own legs, so

I think I'll use yours instead.' Those with gout, the constitution of a scrofulous poet, advanced lethargy, or a tendency towards mega-lomania can all benefit from such an understanding. The one-on-one sedan is the most dramatic illustration of this principle (Fig. 2).

> In Humboldt's *American Researches* he wrote of traversing the Quindin Pass of the Codilleras: 'As few persons in easy circumstances travel on foot in the climate through roads so difficult, during fifteen or twenty days together they are carried by men on a chair, tied on their back; for in the present state of the passage of Quindin it would be impossible to go on mules.'
>
> *A Book about Travelling*, Thomas A. Croal, 1877

Fig. 2   *Walking about can be a tedious business and those who can afford it may wish to employ someone to do the leg-work for them. Variations on this theme include a) the sedan chair, b) the palanquin, c) the surprisingly intimate 'chair strapped to the back of a native' set-up*

Common decency would seem to dictate that those suffering from 'big bones' or morbid obesity should think twice before becoming a passenger on a sedan chair, but, unfortunately, fat people are notoriously selfish and rarely give a second thought to the feelings of others.

> There is a man of the province of Antisquia who is so bulky that he has not met with more than two mulattoes capable of carrying him, and if either of the men had died while he was on the banks of the Magdalena he never could have reached his home!
>
> *A Book about Travelling*, Thomas A. Croal, 1877

And it seems that a fellow need not be miles from civilisation to abuse the good natures of others. A letter from Lord Carlisle to George Selwyn in the late eighteenth century shows a slightly complacent attitude towards the humble chair-carrier – even in such a great man.

> You get up at nine, play with your dog till twelve, then creep down to White's, are five hours at table; sleep till supper time, and then make two wretches carry you in a sedan chair, with three pints of claret in you, three miles for a shilling.
>
> *Letter* from Lord Carlisle, c.1770

A bulky customer should at least compensate his bearers for any inconvenience caused by adding 1 per cent to his tip for every pound overweight he happens to be. With this quid pro quo in place there is no reason why a fellow should not relax and indulge in a jolly decent lunch once in a while. However, it is this question of human rights coupled with the relative inefficiency of the sedan chair which has made it fall out of favour in recent times.

Horse-Drawn Vehicles

The horse-drawn vehicle is another ancient form of conveyance, but the advent of the internal combustion engine has largely put the kibosh on its popular usage in the West. This is rather sad,

Fig. 3

because to my mind the carriage should be promoted as a more natural and stylish alternative to the unspeakable vulgarity of the stretch limo. Neither is without its drawbacks. For instance, it is true that both produce noxious emissions: whilst those from the motor-car travel upwards, potentially doing untold damage to the ozone layer, those from the horse travel down, potentially doing untold damage to a pair of highly-buffed Oxfords. So environmentally it is pretty much a toss-up as to which is the worse offender.

At its best the interior of a carriage should resemble a well-appointed and fashionable drawing room. It should always be borne in mind though, that just as sitting for hours on end in one's favourite chair engrossed in a novel can lead to pressure sores, carriage travel also has its attendant health risks, such as haemorrhoids, dropsy and friction burns.

> If a person is weakly, or undertakes a long excursion, it is then most advisable to travel in a carriage, which may be so ingeniously contrived as to be rendered a magazine of comforts. When travelling by carriage, it is very beneficial occasionally to change our position; that is, to sit sometimes toward one side, and sometimes to the other, and sometimes to recline, &c. By these means, one can best prevent those evils attending continued riding, which are occasioned by the jolting being in one direction.
>
> *The Traveller's Oracle*, Dr William Kitchiner, 1827

꧁ *The Lost Art of Travel* ꧂

The ever-present danger of chafing is not the only hazard that one has to face when travelling. Prolonged journeys in any kind of carriage will often be accompanied by other infirmities too:

> *Sickness from the Motion of a Carriage Prevented* – some persons are so delicately organised that riding for any distance in a coach or carriage induces sickness with them; this may be prevented by holding fast to the side of the carriage, which prevents the body swaying forward with the motion of the carriage.
>
> *Hardships in Travel Made Easy*, 1864

Dr Flünkduster, the eminent shrew expert, is also renowned for being a particularly bad traveller. I do not think I am betraying any confidences when I relate that during one particularly rough journey he clung to the side of the carriage so vehemently that it took almost an hour to prise his fingers from the vehicle after we had arrived at our destination. It is sometimes unwise to take seemingly helpful travel advice too literally.

Of course, these days the once-widespread infrastructure of inns, stables, grooms, etc. for looking after horses has virtually disappeared in cities. Disappointingly, new-build housing estates provide very little by way of stable blocks, and if you do purchase a carriage, staff will have to be trained from scratch and closely supervised.

> While on the road, caution your servant never to trust the cleaning of the carriage to the stablemen of the inn, who, in their careless hurry, and with their old ragged mops and dirty cloths, may scratch and deface the panels more in a few minutes, than with proper care they would suffer in many months: therefore, however you may be obliged to pay these persons their customary perquisites – tell him to look after your carriage and horses himself.
>
> *The Traveller's Oracle*, Dr William Kitchiner, 1827

The public stagecoach is also sadly no more, but you might be amazed to find how the following advice can equally be made to apply to travel in the airless interior of a modern day train, plane, taxi or omnibus.

People are generally anxious to secure front places, either because they cannot, or fancy they cannot ride backwards; but if they travel at night, the wind and rain, while sitting in front, will beat into their faces, the only remedy for which is to draw up the glasses (a privilege vested by travelling etiquette in the occupiers of those places), and thus must they sit the remainder of the night in an atmosphere too impure for any gentleman who has not previously served an apprenticeship in the exhausted receiver of an air pump.

Nothing occasions more severe colds, &c. than the sudden exposure to the cold air immediately after coming out of one of these vapour baths.

Should a person, in travelling for any considerable distance, and sitting backwards, meet with companions who close the windows, and pertinaciously persist in prohibiting any importation of oxygen – if all arguments on the necessity of ventilation are unavailing, and your lungs feel oppressed from the lack of fresh air – you may let your stick or your umbrella fall (accidentally) against one of the windows; i.e., if you are of the opinion that it is more advisable to give a glazier 3s to replace a pane of glass, than it is to pay double that sum for physic to remove a pain in your head, which you will otherwise get by breathing foul air.

Fig. 4

The Traveller's Oracle, Dr William Kitchiner, 1827

Those who are easily irritated by fellow passengers may prefer to take the reins into their own hands and purchase a vehicle made for two (Fig. 4), but being open to scrutiny on the public highway does demand adherence to a strict code of etiquette (especially when travelling with a lady) that involves advanced skills such as the ability to steer a carriage and doff one's hat at the same time.

> If it is reprehensible to smoke when driving with a woman, it is equally under-bred under these circumstances for a driver, however capable his horses may be, to force them to their highest speed and to race them against those of some other driver; also to fail to lift his hat when his companion bows. Should his hands be too full to permit the lifting of his hat, it is enough for him to touch his brim with the stock of his whip. This is accepted always in lieu of the more ceremonious salute; and not only when passing friends of his own or of his companion's on the highway must the hat be touched, but also when right of way is accorded him by any one driving ahead on the same turnpike.
>
> *Encyclopaedia of Etiquette*, Emily Holt, 1901

Cycling

The popularity of the Tour de France (originally conceived of in 1903 as a publicity stunt to sell copies of *L'Auto* newspaper) has added commercial and competitive elements to the art of cycling that many traditionalists heartily disapprove of. Yet still, cycling remains one of the very best ways of keeping the capillaries free from constriction and, on the Continent especially, where road conditions suit, a handy implement of conveyance for touring far and wide. Many experts attest to the health benefits of cycling.

> In my opinion there is no exercise more healthful, or which tends more to ward off disease than cycling. This is particularly the case with regard to both gouty and rheumatic affections. I have also found the exercise very beneficial to people in the first stages of decline and consumption – I prescribe the tricycle instead of a tonic.
>
> Dr Ausrin Meldon, 1878

* * *

Touring is the backbone of cycling, and nothing can surpass the pleasure and exhilaration of wandering free as the wind o'er hill and dale, with no care and anxiety but to drink in the fresh air and sunshine, to feast the eyes on Nature's beauties, and feel in every vein and sinew the throbbing and power of vigorous manhood.

Fig. 5

The Art and Pastime of Cycling,
Richard Mecredy, 1880

The novice, curious to take up cycling for the first time and discover what all the ballyhoo is about, will be brimming with questions, such as: Are people over fifty capable of cycling? Will the velocity of the bicycle prove injurious to my eyesight? Is cycling quite 'natural'? &c. Launching oneself onto a two-wheeled iron frame perfectly capable of reaching speeds up to fifteen miles per hour is not for the faint-hearted and those afflicted by a nervous disposition may want to consider experimenting with the tricycle (Fig. 6) before attempting to master her less equilibrious two-wheeled sister. But beware:

The Tricycle – The general public labour under the impression that any body can ride a tricycle, and most beginners start with this idea. They are sadly mistaken, however, as most beginners soon find out to their cost. In fact, the worst falls are often sustained off the lowly three-wheeler. The novice who attempts to master the narrow-gauger

> has a due regard for the magnitude of the under-
> taking and lays his plans accordingly, with the
> result that he often learns without a single
> fall. The novice who tackles the three-
> wheeler has a lordly disregard for his
> mount, and is convinced
> that he has nothing to do
> but get on and ride away;
> and this over-confidence
> often leads to disaster.
>
> *The Art and Pastime of*
> *Cycling*, Richard Mecredy,
> 1880

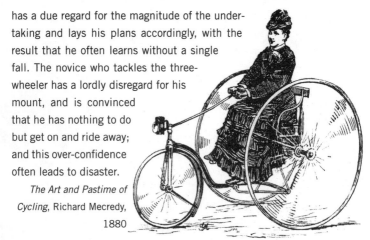

Those new to cycling should also be aware of a curious phenomenon that occurs as

Fig. 6 *Those taking to the road for the first time ought to be careful not to get carried away by the heady excitement of it all*

soon as one attempts to travel downhill. Especially on steep inclines, the rider will find that his feet involuntarily leave the pedals, and his legs will splay out either side of the bicycle at a jaunty diagonal. At the same time he will hear himself emitting an involuntarily high-pitched 'wheeee!' Physics has not yet come up with a plausible explanation why this should happen, but it may have something to do with the dramatic G-forces that are imposed upon the groin region when travelling at high speed. A very tight pair of elasticated under-briefs can go some way to alleviating this condition.

If you still feel up the task, here are some general tips for problem areas that the beginner should keep in mind on their first dozen outings.

Brakes – The learner should make himself acquainted with the working of the brake, for on this his safety may depend. Our first attempt on a tricycle has left a most lively impression on our mind. We started to ride down a moderate incline, without making ourselves acquainted with the working of the brake. The machine was a rear-steering 'Cheylesmore', a type of tricycle, now extinct, upon which the rider could not back-pedal, and half way down the pace became unpleasantly fast, but we could not check it, and swerving and swaying from side to side, we reached the bottom after several hair-breadth escapes.

Corners – This is the rock on which most beginners come to grief. They ride at a corner at eight or ten miles an hour, and when they depart from a direct course the centrifugal force carries them outside the wheel base, and over they go, and the machine is blamed instead of the stupidity of the rider.

The Mouth – The mouth should always be kept shut. The nose is the proper organ to breathe through, and is provided with blood vessels to warm the incoming air, and with minute hairs to catch particles of dust, germs of infection, and other extraneous matter. By breathing through the nose the danger of getting cold, and of contracting lung diseases, is greatly diminished. This, of course, is applicable to everybody, but nose-breathing appeals to the cyclist especially. To ride with an open mouth, besides giving an idiotic appearance [Fig. 7], is apt to cause severe cold, neuralgia, &c. in winter, and in summer the air parches the throat, and renders frequent potations almost necessary, and the small particles of dust are carried into the lungs, and may do great injury.

Pace – A moderate and uniform pace is the most enjoyable. No one should over-exhaust or overheat himself, and should he happen to get overheated he should take great care not to get a chill, or the consequences may prove fatal.

The Art and Pastime of Cycling, Richard Mecredy, 1880

Fig. 7

Once the basic skills have been mastered and you have started to take your new skills seriously, it is time to invest in a range of clothing items suited to the vagaries of weather and the demands of vigorous exertion.

Drawers – If possible, these should be dispensed with, but in the case of many it will be found necessary to wear such during winter. They should be of very light woollen stockinet, and they should not be left off in the spring until the west winds go and the weather becomes decidedly milder. The Jaeger combination of shirt (or chemise) and drawers, in one piece, is a very convenient garment for cycling, as nothing can get out of place.

Trousers – The misguided individual who cycles in trousers suffers in comfort and health. We have long fought against this senseless and unsightly mode of clothing the legs.

Fig. 8

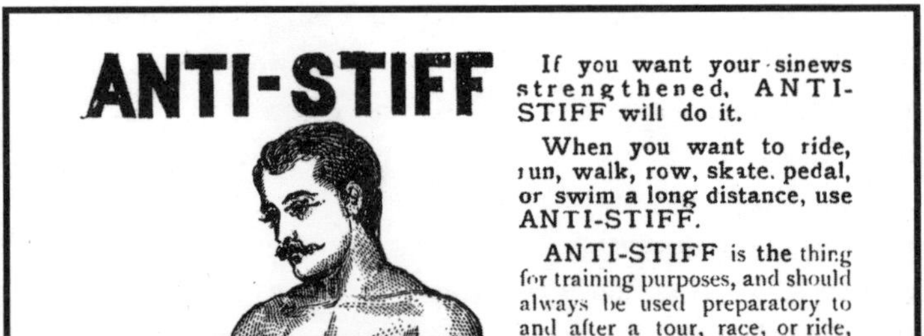

Knee-Breeches – Knee-breeches, when well-made, are more comfortable and neater that knickerbockers. They should fit closely, but should not be too tight, and great care should be taken that they do not grip the knees at any time when riding.

Head Gear – The wide-awake and deer stalker, with good wide brim and of light colour, will be found most serviceable. The helmet, though peculiar looking, is most satisfactory, especially in hot weather. . . . On reaching the halting place for the night, the clothes should be changed, and a cold bath and a good rub down with Elliman's Embrocation or 'Anti-Stiff' [Fig. 8] will refresh one wonderfully and remove all stiffness.

The Art and Pastime of Cycling, Richard Mecredy, 1880

Rickshaws

Worth a brief mention, the rickshaw was first observed in the late 1860s in Yokohama as the jin-riki-sha or jinricksha (literally meaning 'man-powered vehicle'). This love child of the bicycle and the sedan chair comes in two basic forms: the traditional foot-powered arrangement (Fig. 9) and its more modern pedal-driven variety. Potential passengers of runner-pulled rickshaws should always demand that their runner is stylishly illustrated with body art prior to departure (Fig. 10).

As soon as you are seated, the man, who generally divests himself of all clothing, showing a body beautifully tattooed, gets between the shafts, lifts them off the ground and raising the crossbar even with his breast, pushes the carriage along with his hands, going over the flat roads at a great pace.

Fig. 9

J.F. Campbell quoted in *A Book about Travelling*, Thomas A. Croal, 1877

Fig. 10

Having such a fellow running before one can be as aesthetically satisfying as a trip to the Oriental Prints section of the British Museum, but it is advisable to blindfold one's wife for the duration of the journey. If Mrs Darkwood is anything to go by, the sight of decorated male buttocks has a tendency to make ladies gape and become quite breathless – in a state of frozen disapproval. It is a kindness to spare them such needless suffering.

Railway

The invention of the railway engine must be regarded as one of the greatest blessings of the modern traveller, but unless you are fortunate enough to have your own personal fleet of liveried Pullman coaches, train travel does entail some unpleasant communal aspects that may not suit the squeamish.

There was a time when a train passenger knew exactly where he stood. He chose from: 1st Class – expensive and exclusive; 2nd Class – cheap, but not entirely respectable; or 3rd Class – suitable only for riffraff. Now, in more egalitarian times, the demarcation line between carriages is becoming increasingly blurred (a paper antimacassar pinned to the back of a seat is sometimes the only indication that you have reached a superior compartment), no one is pampered and no one brutalised, and consequently all disembark a train feeling slightly cheated without knowing precisely why.

The best plan is to engage, where possible, a sleeper cabin, so that at least you will have recourse to your own private cupboard if you get weary of the throng. More sociable passengers should engage a seat in a first-class compartment, being sure not to stint on making themselves as comfortable as possible.

Take your seat with your back to the engine, as this not only causes the motion to be less felt, but prevents the ashes from the tender flying into your eyes through the open windows. Should you be compelled to sit with your face to the engine you should wear a pair of spectacles made expressly for railway travelling. Having taken your seat . . . make yourself up comfortably for the journey. To promote this, be provided with a rug to wrap round your legs, and a cap that fits closely to the head, and has a band on either side to protect the ears [Fig. 11], button your coat over your chest, place a travel bag or parcel beneath your feet, and you will be quite prepared for the undertaking.

Fig. 11 *Some thought should be given to the selection of clothing designed to stave off the worst effects of public transport*

Hardships in Travel Made Easy, 1864

Hearty types wishing to indulge in a little amateur anthropology might wish to chance dabbling with lower class accommodation, but a few simple ruses will have to be employed to make it a moderately bearable experience.

The art of making himself comfortable is a valuable qualification for a traveller. I sit at the engine end in the long foreign third-class carriages so as to get a good view of the company and to avoid getting coal grit in my eyes – and in a long journey I put on my slippers and a light raincoat instead of my coat and waistcoat. In the dusty trains in Java the Dutchmen bathe their faces with eau-de-cologne mixed with water and an evening train-headache can be dispelled by laying a handkerchief dipped in lavender water across the forehead. An air-cushion half blown up lessens the hardness of the wooden seats and provides amusement for your fellow-passengers.

The Happy Traveller, Revd Frank Tatchell, 1923

Fig. 12

Those who do meddle with the natural order of things, and, in pursuit of local colour and authenticity decide to travel in second- or even third-class carriages only have themselves to blame if things go horribly awry.

The great majority of native passengers travel third-class, most of the remainder second-class, while only a few, principally persons of wealth and distinction, travel first class. All Europeans, excepting soldiers, artisans, etc., are expected to travel first class.

I remember on one occasion making a night journey of some 200 miles in a second-class compartment, and the impression left by my sufferings will not be easily effaced . . . Not foreseeing a crowd, I had installed myself on the bench farthest from the engine, laying down rug and cushions, and fondly looking forward to a comfortable as well as inexpensive journey; but at every succeeding station fresh native passengers dropped in, with bundles, baskets, boxes, bunches of plantains, etc., and the carriage gradually filled; first one bench and then another, had its full complement of occupants, until at last my domain began to be encroached upon. First one sleek Hindu, then another, then a couple more, closed in upon me, till cushions, rugs, etc., had to be bundled up, and I was finally reduced to being one of a row.

Modes of Conveyance

I am imbued with no instinctive repugnance to Hindus or Asiatics in general . . . At the same time, I must admit, that my cosmopolitan leanings were put to a severe trial upon this occasion.

Many of the natives are addicted to practices which make them anything but agreeable *compagnons de voyage* in close quarters. In the first place, they lubricate the body with oil, sometimes cocoanut, but often castor or margosa oil; the two latter kinds have a most foetid and, to a European, a most disgusting and nauseating smell. Secondly, being often fat, the natives perspire very freely, which they can hardly be blamed for, but which intensifies the effect of the anointment . . .

But worst of all, is their habit of eructating on all occasions, without the least attempt at restraint. Nothing is more surprising to an Englishman, accustomed to look on such an act as a gross breach of good manners; but the natives argue, that after a substantial meal, this is an appropriate method of venting their satisfaction – as it were by way of grace.

The European in India, Edmund Hull, 1878

These days, unless you are travelling on some specially organised *voyage gastronomique*, it is unwise to expect anything by way of decent victuals aboard a train. The traveller is advised to equip himself with a capacious hamper stuffed to the gunwales with every imaginable delicacy. In many countries, hawkers of all kinds will board trains at stations and offer passengers local fare (Fig. 13). Purchasing such food always entails a certain level of risk, but a traveller soon becomes adept at spotting suspicious commodities. For instance, a boiled guinea pig wrapped in brown paper bought from a Peruvian peasant woman may well prove surprisingly palatable, whilst anything clad in plastic and proffered by an acned trolley-pusher on a train in England is almost guaranteed to be inedible and should be avoided at all costs.

Some passengers disgruntled by a long journey may seek solace in the bottle. Others may become fractious. If your fellow

Fig. 13 *Hawkers giving every appearance of unwashed ne'er-do-wells may actually provide surprisingly palatable victuals*

travellers prove unpleasant it is inadvisable to attempt any amateur heroics.

If a person is intoxicated, abusive, or otherwise misconducts himself, call the guard and have him removed, instead of wasting your time and temper in endeavouring to remonstrate with him. Do not take your seat in a carriage which is already occupied by a party of friends or acquaintances, the feeling of being 'one too many,' with which you will afterwards become impressed, is extremely unpleasant and irksome.

Hardships in Travel Made Easy, 1864

If you do have to throw your lot in with total strangers, instead of remaining aloof, time can be made to pass more pleasantly by engaging fellow passengers in various parlour games. Nothing is calculated to break the ice more effectively than attempting to pass a ping-pong ball around the compartment from chin to chin, or, alternatively, a rumbustious game of Twister. Card games such as Split Giblet, Macedonian Whist and Crump also go down particularly well on long journeys.

Apart from dealing with fellow passengers, there will be the little matter of travel servants to contend with. Taking personal staff aboard trains is slightly problematical these days, as cut-price tickets for servants no longer seem to be railway policy. On modern trains, if you wish to take staff, it is best to check them in

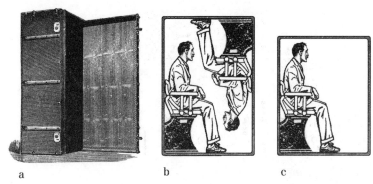

Fig. 14   *The Bentley & Simpkins servant transporters – ideal for the economical conveyance of staff. Comprising (a) sturdy leather exterior, (b) cost-effective double-decker model, (c) deluxe single for added comfort*

as luggage. Most servants are happy enough to go along with this arrangement, because if they decide to travel as a passenger their fare is generally deducted from their wage-packet. Bentley & Simpkins do a sumptuous range of servant transporters (Fig. 14). In my experience the single transporter, whilst wasting a certain amount of space, is by far the most convenient, as the double-decker model does require turning every half an hour to alleviate the blood pressure on the inverted servant's brain. On one journey this proved impossibly inconvenient, as Stourbridge (far too useful to pack) was sitting in as fourth man in a game of bridge, but had to toddle off every thirty minutes or so to give the luggage a turn.

Motor Car

As with most things in life, the art of driving is 80 per cent confidence and appearance.

> The driver should endeavour to cultivate a comfortable appearance at the wheel, which is not merely a matter of looks, as in addition to appearing at home with his work – and therefore calm and collected as a good driver should be – it is an attitude likely to encourage the

actual obtaining of such a desirable state of affairs. Many car drivers have a nervous appearance, which gives a bad impression from the mere point of view of looks and does not promise well for actual fact. The capable driver usually has the appearance of being as much at home at the seat of the car which he is driving as one would expect to find him when comfortably ensconced in an armchair by his own fireside [Fig. 15].

Fig. 15

How to Drive a Motorcar, The Motor magazine, 1914

Whilst important, looking good is not a foolproof guarantee that a driver will also be safe and proficient. Apart from the requisite manual skills, a potential motorist should attempt to hone his senses to the animal acuity of a bird of prey.

Well-trained eyes are an all-abounding fount of security . . . Few drivers, it is to be feared, have made a point of training their eyes. The eye itself is a remarkably complex piece of the human anatomy, yet its powers of observation can undoubtedly be improved by scientific training.

How to Drive a Motorcar, The Motor magazine, 1914.

One of the best ways I have found of training the eyes is to sit for hours on end in a cinema with one's head turned sideways to the screen trying to follow the action merely by using one's peripheral vision. Another good technique, invented by Colonel Pearce, is to get a friend to drive a golf ball at you side on and attempt to dodge it (Fig. 16). The substitution of a bat and cricket ball for more advanced pupils, gives greater motivation to avoid being hit.

The cultivation of quick thinking is also tremendously important too:

> The driver should train his eyes to picture not only probabilities but also possibilities. Take the case of a pedestrian apparently wandering aimlessly in the centre of the road. Now, although it is done probably 99 times out of 100, and although one may advance sound arguments that it is excusable, nevertheless it should not, in point of fact, be argued by the driver that because he sounds his horn the said pedestrian will move to the side of the road.
>
> The trained eye naturally assumes the very strong possibility of such a thing happening, but has a glimmering vision as to the possibility of that person being deaf, hopelessly 'in the moon,' stupid, or even drunk.
>
> *How to Drive a Motorcar, The Motor* magazine, 1914

Fig. 16 *There are various ways of improving one's peripheral vision, but ideally the driver should choose a method that strongly reinforces the need for quick reactions in response to dangerous situations . . .*

Pedestrians (in addition to corners and trees) are undoubtedly the bane of all motorists. It is quite amazing how, once you are behind the wheel, all members of the public seem to become so many skittles tempting the driver to run them down. If this image starts to become an obsession then it is just possible that driving is not

Fig. 17

for you, but such thoughts can be dispelled by the consumption of a bottle of wine and a couple of Valium before driving – although the calming effect of such medication can lead to drowsiness.

> The writer has had experience of drivers falling asleep on more than one occasion, and once when on a long night journey, entirely given up to the charms of Morpheus on the back seat, suddenly awoke to find himself with torn clothes and scratched face and hands, in the middle of a hedge. The explanation was that the driver, who was a thoroughly moderate man in every way, and healthier and stronger physically than ninety-nine men out of a hundred, had fallen asleep, the car had jumped the grass curb, and he awoke only in time to assist in stopping the car when its progress was mainly arrested by the hedge.
>
> *How to Drive a Motorcar*, 1914

Even if you are fully awake, there will always be circumstances that take the motorist unawares. If you anticipate a particularly difficult drive it is only sensible to designate a driver genetically suited to the task.

> In these 'suffragette' days one hesitates even to offer any advice to ladies, but as the whole of the writer's experience with lady drivers

has tended to lead to one set conclusion, it is deemed advisable to briefly touch on the subject . . . There are certain situations in which one finds it impossible to concede that the average lady driver is the equal of the average male. The whole of the conditions referred to may be summed up in the one word 'emergencies'.

There is something in the construction of human beings which varies with the sex, allowing the mere male to act more quickly in any surprise engendered by an emergency than one of the gentler sex.

How to Drive a Motorcar, The Motor magazine, 1914

As an extra safeguard, drivers may wish to consider equipping their cars with a set of pedestrian repellent rollers that automatically drop to the ground when contact is made with an obstacle (Fig. 18). Then if they are unable to hit the brake in time then at least pedestrians can be harmlessly swept away from the front of the car, without doing serious damage either to themselves or, more importantly, to the headlights and paintwork of the vehicle.

Young men can have a tendency to revert to big foolish children when it comes to motor cars. There is something about polished chrome, bright shiny paintwork, walnut veneer and an excessively loud horn, that takes its toll on a man's sense of reason and turns him into a frenzied velocity junkie. Careering around country

Fig. 18   *Pedestrian repellent rollers – the only truly effective way of reducing the dangers posed by the unwary motorist.*

lanes at speeds topping 30 miles per hour may be fleetingly impressive to some blonde piece that you have just met in the saloon bar of the Dog and Duck, but is unlikely to hold much sway with people of substance.

> Never allow yourself to become addicted to the bad practice of showing off. For instance, there is nothing particularly clever in causing the rear wheel to spin round at a great speed and so cause a shower of sparks from the steel-studded non-skid tyre when starting up. Neither is there anything particularly clever in driving up to a traffic block or other necessary stoppage at a high speed and then jamming on the brakes so as to effect a spectacular stop.
>
> *How to Drive a Motorcar, The Motor* magazine, 1914

Camels

Apart from Ernest Memling, my old theology tutor, the camel is without doubt the most absurd-looking creature known to man; but by some strange corruption of the laws of aesthetics it somehow contrives to appear graceful and romantic when spied sauntering across the arid lands of north Africa (which is more than can be said for Mr Memling).

Lesson number one is how to get on the blighter:

> The traveller should of course learn to ride a camel before under-taking journeys of any length. He will at first only mount when the camel is kneeling, but will learn quickly 'to mount by the neck' of a standing camel. To do this, the rider stands on the beast's near side and with the right hand grips the front edge of the *makhlufa*; his left hand rest on the back of the camel's neck. From this position the rider jumps and pulls himself up so that the left knee rests beside the left hand on the camel's neck and the right leg hangs straight. The right knee is then brought up so that the rider is kneeling on the camel's neck. He then places the left foot on the neck, shifting his right hand to the fore-post (*el-'amud*) of the *makhlufa*, and so clambers into the saddle. The rider ought, until well practiced, to have a care least he

injure himself seriously on the *'amud.'*

Handbook of Travel, The Harvard Travellers' Club, 1917

Fig. 19

Once comfortably mounted, a few basic techniques on manoeuvring the beast will also come in handy. Unlike a motor car there are no complicated levers, luminous dials or confusing switches to master. In fact, all one needs is a modicum of intuition and an innate understanding of animal psychology, together with a brief course in camel-speak and a smattering of mesmerism.

Camels do not bite or kick (except when they must), but they can give a violent sneeze of half-masticated cud, which is almost as bad. With them *oos, oos* means go on; *adda* turn; *ogf* stop; and *ch ch ch*, lie down. They are the only animal in the world to move the legs of one side before the others move.

The Happy Traveller, Revd Frank Tatchell, 1923

* * *

It is seldom advisable to beat a camel with a stick; more can be done by whirling the camel stick in a circle a few inches above the beast's head.

Handbook of Travel, The Harvard Travellers' Club, 1917

Dealing with a camel does require some natural authority, however. If you are one of those people who constantly find themselves cornered by small dogs or mocked by young children in the street, then maybe you should think about engaging a more docile species of animal.

Elephants

Elephants are generally even-tempered beasts, and particularly easy to deal with, as their management is left entirely to an experienced mahout. All the same, it is just as well to arm yourself with a few nuggets of expertise when buying an elephant, to avoid being imposed upon by an unscrupulous salesman. Interestingly enough, a badly bred elephant exhibits precisely the same telltale warning signs that one looks out for when selecting a new pantry boy.

> Marks of inferior breeding – eyes restless; hair of head mixed shades; face wrinkled; tongue curved and black; nails short and green; ears small; neck thin; skin freckled; forehead lean and low.
>
> *A Manual of the Diseases of the Elephant*, John Steele, 1885

Fig. 20 *In a face-off between an elephant and a hen it is tempting to assume that the pachyderm might have the upper hand. But feet like tree trunks and razor-sharp tusks are apparently no match for beady eyes full of menace*

Modes of Conveyance

As with the camel, when riding on such a large animal, possibly for days at a stretch, it is useful to equip yourself with some knowledge of the temperament of the beast. Most elephants exhibit a feebleness of intellect and lack of moral fibre.

> The habits of the elephant are very simple, but strange to say are not generally known, most popular ideas about him being sentimental and fictitious. His mental and moral qualities are in the main such as are suited to render him useful as a working animal . . . He has very little courage, for although at times he will fight well, against other elephants or tigers for instance, he is somewhat deficient in pluck as a rule, bolts from the sound of fire arms, and has been put to rout even by such a small animal as a dog. Indeed he objects to most small animals – dogs, pigs, and such like – and is said to have an uncon-querable dislike for poultry [Fig. 20]. He is apt to be boisterously playful at times and by a sudden broadside charge at a laden elephant to send him sprawling on the ground.
>
> *A Manual of the Diseases of the Elephant*, John Steele, 1885

Similarly to infirm relatives, elderly neighbours and small children, elephants can prove an utter nuisance in the evening, when stimulating conversation and partying must be kept to the minimum in order to let the blighters get a decent night's sleep.

> There should be strict silence in the *filkhana* after 9.30 p.m. as by that time most of the elephants will have filled themselves and will lie down and sleep.
>
> *A Manual of the Diseases of the Elephant*, John Steele, 1885

An elephant deprived of adequate repose can become exceedingly crotchety in the morning. A riled elephant, much like an infuriated sumo wrestler, is an absurd and even comical sight to the Western eye, but one should never underestimate the damage potential of a creature with quite so much weight to throw around. Curiously, the technique for subduing a stroppy elephant is similar to the enlightened and compassionate way we in the

West deal with particularly awkward inmates in old people's homes and mental institutions.

> A dangerous man killer can be reduced to temporary harmlessness by a daily pill of opium and hemp.
>
> *A Manual of the Diseases of the Elephant*, John Steele, 1885

All in all, though, one has to admit that relying on animals as transport is reasonably high-maintenance compared to mechanical means.

Ballooning

For some reason the balloon has gained a reputation for being the most romantic form of travel known to man. This is possibly due to the fact that as a practical means of transport it is also singularly useless. Ever since the Mongolfier brothers started their eccentric experiments in the 1780s (Fig. 21), the balloon has proved largely unsteerable, desperately slow, at the mercy of wind currents and storms, and limited in passenger space. The hot air balloon is therefore chiefly suitable for surveying, meteorology, anti-aircraft purposes, or, alternatively, just having a bit of a lark.

Fig. 21

> In theory no experience that we poor non-flying mortal can enjoy is more fascinating, more ideally charming, more poetically sublime, than a trip heavenward in that curious, unnatural, and yet extremely simple apparatus – a balloon. To soar aloft, rising up and up without rocking or vibration. To glide o'er the country,

above the tree-tops and houses, perfectly noiselessly, perfectly at ease. To gaze on distant views, on glorious cloudscapes, and have the earth laid flat beneath one's feet.

Ballooning as a Sport, Major B. Baden-Powell, 1907

Women are hormonally programmed to be impressed by males who show a certain amount of dash, and in the modern world this commodity is usually made manifest by an impressively bushy moustache, a shiny red sports cars or a large private income. Right at the top of the dash stakes, however, is being the owner of a hot air balloon. If impressing the ladies is your aim, then it is imperative that you make sure you know the sport of ballooning inside out. Nothing can be more detrimental to a fledgling romance than finding yourself hanging lopsidedly from a tree or plunging head first into a ditch as the climax of your first date. The safety of the basket is of paramount importance.

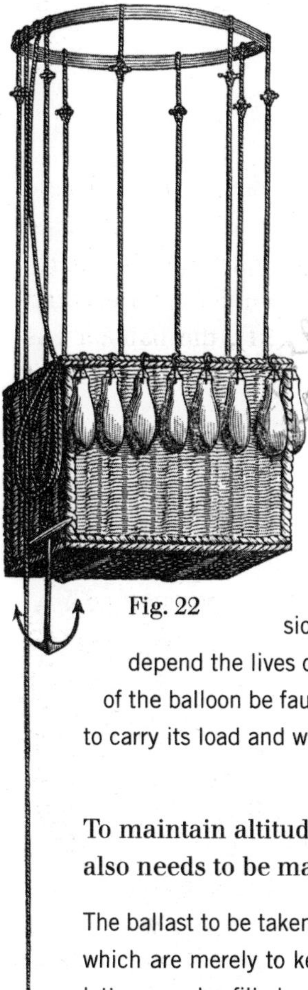

Fig. 22

The basket is to be made by a professional [Fig. 22], as upon its workmanship may depend the lives of its occupants, though every other feature of the balloon be faultless. It must be light, and still very strong to carry its load and withstand severe bumping.

How to Fly, Richard Ferris, 1910

To maintain altitude, the skill of 'chucking stuff overboard' also needs to be mastered.

The ballast to be taken must be kept distinct from the sand-bags, which are merely to keep the balloon down during inflation. The latter may be filled with any coarse stuff, but the former must contain only fine, well-sifted sand, so as not to do any damage if dropped on people or housetops.

Ballooning as a Sport, Major
B. Baden-Powell, 1907

As indicated, ballast should always consist of fine sand, but in an emergency it is permissible to jettison suitcases, seats, medical kits, or, if need be, pets and staff, in an attempt to gain height. Simple ballooning etiquette stipulates that a letter of apology and an offer of compensation should be sent to anyone who sustains injury to their person, property or livestock from objects hurtling down upon them.

Fig. 23 *The mark of a true professional is the suavity and aplomb with which he brings his craft back down to earth*

After several hours of drifting aimlessly about in the blue yonder it will suddenly occur to you what a colossal waste of time it is to spend a valuable afternoon suspended over the countryside in an over-sized picnic hamper and you will no doubt be grasped by a fervent impulse to return to ground. On a descent it is frightfully important to locate a few simple yokels who can be relied upon to pack up your gear and carry it for you to the nearest mini-cab office or railway station.

When, from the ballast getting short or darkness coming on or other cause, it is deemed desirable to make a landing [Fig. 23], there are two or three matters to be considered. It is generally convenient to come down not too far from a railway station, so that the map and the railway guide must be brought into requisition. Then it is most necessary to have some assistance, so wait till you see people about before descending. But it more often occurs that the circumstances are all the other way, and that there are too many people. You don't want a crowd, therefore avoid the proximity of a large town.

Ballooning as a Sport, Major B. Baden-Powell, 1907

On no account alight on territory where you suspect that the locals will lack sympathy with your vocation as an adventurer. When Professor Charles sent up an experimental balloon from the Champ de Mars, Paris in 1783 he had little inkling of the hostile reception it would receive on returning back to Earth:

It fell in a rural region near Paris, where it was totally destroyed by the inhabitants, who believed it to be some hideous form of the devil.

How to Fly, Richard Ferris, 1910

Of course, the only truly practical way to travel by air is in an aeroplane, but due to the increasing vulgarity of this mode of transport I have purposely left it out of our considerations here. My few forays into powered flight have convinced me that it has no place in the repertoire of the modern traveller, and apart from the escapades of the early pioneers or the bracing novelty of wing-walking on a bi-plane, I remain to be convinced that a true adventurer should ever succumb to its dubious charms.

Boat

When leaving British shores it is traditionally most stylish to depart from Dover, Southampton or Liverpool by sailing ship or cruise liner. As with all modes of communal transport, travelling first-class will usually ensure that the traveller need not put too much thought into the endeavour, apart from determining the appropriate dress for promenading the deck (Fig. 24) or the correct form of address when chatting with the captain or any nobility who may happen to be on board.

Fig. 24

> 'Good morning' and 'good evening' and a slight graceful bow serve as sufficient introduction to one's travelling companions. At table, on deck, in the corridors, library and drawing room it is permissible to venture to speak to other passengers. Harmless common-places of conversation such as comments on the weather and the ship's run, and the comforts of the vessel lead the way naturally into general talk.
>
> *Encyclopaedia of Etiquette*, Emily Holt, 1901

In fact, the only trouble you are likely to encounter aboard a ship will emanate from one of two sources – either from the sea, or from persons travelling steerage.

> See that it is a fixed regulation of the ship that no smoking is to be allowed, and that no candles or fires are on any account to be permitted, except under the direct regulation and supervision of the officers of the ship. Persons of the working classes are very careless in the carrying of ignited materials, and a drunken man will peril the lives of all [Fig. 25].
>
> . . . A sea-voyage is by no means so formidable an affair as is imaged. To good ships, well found, manned, and efficient, it is amazing how seldom any serious accident happens, and still more remarkable how frequently life is saved in shipwreck. During the early part of the voyage, timid people suffer a good deal from fear; should the wind blow hard, and the sea run high, they will be likely to overrate the danger, especially at night, when the crew are busy reducing sail; the trampling of the sailors overhead, the loud voices of the commander and the mates giving orders, and the careering of the vessel,

Modes of Conveyance

very naturally create alarm. This will be increased by hearing other passengers express their fears. Fear begets fear, and the steerage very often presents a scene of great confusion without the least cause for it.

Hardships in Travel Made Easy, 1864

Generally speaking, though, as long as one avoids tempests and hurricanes, collisions with passing icebergs, foundering on rocky shores, attack by pirates, killer seagulls or giant squid (Fig. 26), scurvy, food poisoning, sea-sickness or on-board epidemics, everything should quite literally be plain sailing. Assuming that you do actually arrive at your destination, when disembarking the vessel you may wish to thank the staff for keeping you, against all odds, out of harm's way.

When leaving the ship: it is only polite to bid adieu to the Captain and officers if anything more than the conventional daily greetings have been exchanged with them. It is also courteous to go about, a little while before the ship reaches her dock, and say good-bye to all those fellow passengers with whom even a passing friendship has been maintained.

Encyclopaedia of Etiquette,
Emily Holt, 1901

Fig. 25 *Members of the working classes can be identified from their dishevelment and a drunkenly lax attitude towards fire*

Alternatively, if you find yourself in the middle of the Indian Ocean bobbing about in an over-crowded lifeboat or, more inconveniently, clinging to a piece of drift-wood, then it is permissible to dispense with the usual

Fig. 26

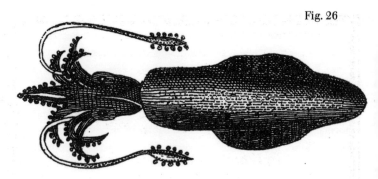

formalities altogether. In the remote likelihood that you are picked up by a passing vessel, a brisk note of complaint and a demand for full reimbursement for the missed portion of the voyage should be sent to the shipping line on return to terra firma.

CHAPTER THE TENTH

In Which Advice is Given on

HEALTH AND HYGIENE

HEALTH AND HYGIENE

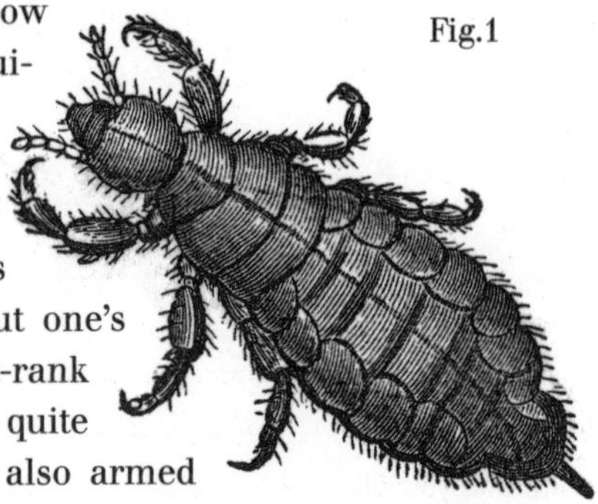

We have already seen how the acquisition of antiquities, exotic recipes and amusing anecdotes can gain quite a reputation for a traveller on his return to civilisation; but one's credibility as a first-rank explorer will never be quite complete unless one is also armed with an impressive catalogue of ailments, parasites, bites, lacerations and infirmities one has suffered from along the way. Any adventurer worth the name should be able to hold a table of dinner-guests in a state of extreme thrall with revolting accounts of tropical diseases, giant insects and narrow escapes from death, authenticating these tales, now and then, by rolling up a trouser leg to reveal a weeping sore or lifting up his shirt to expose an angry multicoloured rash. As a *pièce de résistance* a pillbox may be withdrawn from one's jacket pocket during pudding, containing an entomological sample such as a scorpion, some pubic lice or a small colony of army ants.

Fig.1

Ailments and Diseases

In some respects, surveying the list of illnesses and ailments one is likely to contract when abroad is a bit like visiting Harrods' tea department – the variety can be bewildering. The traveller will no doubt have encountered old favourites such as malaria, prickly heat, ringworm, cholera, schistosoma and Mapucho haemorrhagic fever, but it is sometimes the more prosaic ailments that are likely to act as a continuous source of irritation. Once again lack of space prevents exhaustive analysis, but here are a few of the more common travellers' maladies:

Dysentery – If you catch it in the wilds and have no drugs, chew wood charcoal or scrape a powder from a charred stick and swallow it with water.

Eczema – Live for a week or two on nothing but milk and oranges, with an occasional dose of Epsom salts.

Sea sickness – Try stopping both ears tightly with cotton wool.

Sunstroke – Keep in a darkened room, and after sunset, not before, dissolve a teaspoon of ordinary salt in a wine glassful of cold water. Trickle a little into both ears a drop at a time. This takes away the pain, and you will sink into a delightful sleep and be nearly all right the next day.

Grit in the Eye – Rub the other eye, then both eyes will water. Carry a small camel's hair brush for getting grit out, and after you have done so put a drop of castor oil in the eye . . . Snuff is good for the eyes. The Zulus, who are inveterate snuff-takers, have the finest eyesight in the world.

The Happy Traveller, Revd Frank Tatchell, 1923

With this last affliction in mind, the following counsel may be of further assistance.

Never rub your eyes except with your elbows.

A Handbook for Travellers in Spain, Richard Ford, 1847

I remain to be convinced that this is actually physically possible, but from the point of view of hygiene, I am sure it is eminently sound advice. Unless you are particularly agile, my recommendation is: if your eyes need massaging, then try rubbing them with somebody else's elbows instead (Fig. 2).

Fig. 2

The utility of a dog in the testing of poisoned water has already been alluded to, but that other domestic staple, the cat, can also come in useful. Whilst making a particularly unrewarding pet, the cat can compensate for its inadequacies by providing sterling service to its masters in other ways. If a mountaineer is concerned that he is climbing to heights where altitude sickness is likely to become a problem, then a trusty feline can give him advanced warning of this.

> *Rarified Air* – On high plateaux or mountains, travellers must expect to suffer somewhat. The symptoms are described by many South American travellers; the attack of them is there, among other names, called the puna. The disorder is sometimes fatal to stout plethoric people; oddly enough, cats are unable to endure it. At villages 13,000 feet above the sea, Dr Tscudi says that they cannot live. Numerous trials have been made, but the creatures die in frightful convulsions.
>
> *The Art of Travel*, Francis Galton, 1872

Constipation is renowned as the bane of the over-fifties the moment they attempt to travel further afield than their own front gates. An effective aperient medicine should always be packed and, if home chemistry is your thing, an hour with pestle and

Health and Hygiene

mortar and some easily found household ingredients will ensure
that the infirmities of middle age will not be a worry to you.

> To make forty of Dr Kitchiner's Peristaltic Persuaders:
> - Take Rhubarb finely pulverised, Two drachms;
> - Syrup (by weight), One drachm;
> - Oil of Carraway, Ten drops (Minims).
> - Make forty pills, each of which will contain three grains of
>   Rhubarb.
>
> *The Traveller's Oracle*, Dr William Kitchiner, 1827

An Englishman dwelling abroad is likely to be more vulnerable
to the numerous filthy infections of an unnatural climate than the
natives tend to be. On the whole he is loath to make a fuss about
it, but laid low by fevers and tropical diseases he will be seen
more often than not swooning on a divan on his verandah.
Naturally enough, admiring his master very much and seeing
him thus indisposed, a native's instinct is to emulate him. At times
this can lead to locals imagining that they suffer as we do.

> The imaginary ailments of natives are neither few or far between; but
> it is not at all times wise to disregard them. We have known our fol-
> lowers come, night after night, with small sicknesses, when we had
> but a few doses of fever mixture left, and, by some chance or other,
> a little curry powder. Now, had we sent away a man and his 'little sick-
> ness', he would have been really ill next morning. We therefore looked
> as wise as possible, felt his pulse, looked at his tongue, read a para-
> graph or two, and sent him to boil some water and bring it to us; we
> then carefully measured out a spoonful of curry powder, mixed it, saw
> him drink it off, and sent him to make himself as warm as he could
> till next morning.
>
> *Shifts and Expedients of Camp Life*, Lord and Baines, 1876

On five occasions I have had native porters die from imaginary
ailments. Having complained of pains in the head or abdomen
they are found stiff and cold the following morning, despite
liberal doses of curry powder the night before. Indeed I once

witnessed a man expire from an imaginary snakebite that gave the absolute appearance of being the real thing – his lower leg dark purple and swollen to three times its natural size. The suggestive power of the human mind is truly a remarkable thing.

Insects, Vermin and Other Troublesome Creatures

Mosquitoes

While staying at a hotel overseas, an Englishman can always tell whether his neighbour is a fellow-countryman by a very singular acoustic phenomenon. Whereas the British summer is defined by the characteristic sound of leather on willow, abroad the presence of an Englishman is heralded by the noise of rolled-up newspaper on pillow, plaster, wood, or indeed any other surface where a mosquito may temporarily alight. It is an age-old ritual that the three-quarters of an hour before lights-out be spent pirouetting and leaping about in one's underwear attempting to swat any insect that looks as if it is planning a nocturnal feeding frenzy.

> These troublesome insects invariably torment Europeans in the West Indies, and other warm climates. Their bite produces small tumours, which inflame and itch to such a degree as to cause a continual scratching, and often very troublesome ulcerations. To allay this, it will be necessary frequently to bathe the parts with hartshorn, solution of sugar of lead, or with diluted laudanum; at the same time to cool the body by an occasional dose of Epsom salts.
>
> *Hardships in Travel Made Easy*, 1864

Those who lack the energy to indulge in a pre-emptive cull or those sleeping under canvas may wish to try other techniques of avoiding the attentions of spiteful insects. Quite apart from its bite, the mosquito makes an infuriating high-pitched whine, like a prepubescent doodlebug, that keeps the sleeper awake in fear of imminent attack, but luckily a splendid device invented by

Mr Levinge can ensure a good night's sleep without recourse to chemicals or excessive exertion (Fig. 3).

> Every traveller who is going to the East must, if he values health and comfort, take the sleeping apparatus which is called Levinge's bag . . . The comfort of this bag, to those who are nervous about vermin, or easily annoyed by them, is inestimable. The certainty that one is safe from every intruder tends of itself to give one good nights. The traveller will, of course, see that his bag is never left open for a moment; and that no one is ever allowed to put a hand within it who cannot be trusted for cleanliness.

> *Eastern Life*, Harriet Martineau, 1848

* * *

It is desirable that the traveller should enter this bed as he would a shower-bath, and having his night shirt with him. When the end formed of muslin is suspended, the bed forms an airy canopy in which the occupant may stand up and dress in privacy, no one being able to see him from without, while he can observe all around. To

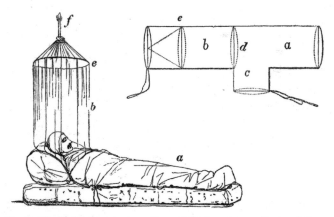

Fig. 3 *The Levinge apparatus – For a night free of mosquitoes and fleas etc., the sleeper enters the canvas bag through entrance (c) but is still able to maintain a look out for bellicose natives and mad dogs through the muslin curtain (b) that surrounds the head during the hours of sleep*

prevent accidents from tearing the apparatus, I have found that the best mode of entering it was to keep the opening in the middle of the mattress, and, standing in it, draw the bag entrance over my head.

During the day the traveller might read and write within it free from the annoyance of flies, and in the evening, by placing a candle near the curtain, he may pursue his occupations undisturbed by gnats . . . Travellers who have used Mr Levinge's contrivance have found it answer to the purpose effectually; it excludes bugs and mosquitoes, and, when carefully managed fleas also.

Murray's Handbook for Travellers in Constantinople, 1871

Fleas

Fig. 4

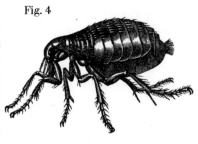

For non-airborne insects the traveller is often left with no viable alternative but to smother his clothes and bedding with powerful insecticides. After such treatment the occupant of a bed should avoid breathing too deeply, opening his eyes or eating in bed. Casually brushing off the DDT from a buttered crumpet accidentally dropped-face-down on sheets can be regarded as neither appetising nor healthful.

Keating's Insect Powder is indispensable. The mats of the rooms at the inns and the quilts which form the bedding, in summer, invariably swarm with fleas and unless some preventative is used, the traveller will probably pass sleepless nights. The best method is to freely sprinkle the inside of the nightdress with the powder; where fleas are particularly annoying, its direct application to the person will be found very effective. A sheet of oiled-paper spread over the quilts before putting on the sheets is some protection, but its unpleasant

smell has often the effect of causing a headache. A little camphore
is sometimes effectual.

Murray's Handbook for Travellers in Central and Northern Japan, 1884

Even during the daytime, it is best to keep one's ankles well
covered when dining at local hostelries.

All parts of the East abound in vermin of every description, each
annoying the weary traveller, and some by their bite occasioning
serious pain or illness; this is particularly the case in wayside coffee
houses, which should be avoided, as they are reputed to contain what
the Turks call, for politeness' sake, black fleas and white fleas: it is
best to sit outside.

Murray's Handbook for Travellers in Constantinople, 1871

If you are forced to patronise such establishments, make sure
that you wear either galoshes, bicycle-clips or a pair of waders
to thwart the migration of fleas and lice up your legs and ultimately via the knees, to the damp recesses of your nether
regions.

Leeches

Another creature that is famous for being an anklophile is the
leech, but in reality this sordid annelid is not in the slightest bit
fussy as to what part of your anatomy it sinks its teeth into. They
have a reputation for dropping from trees, or of lurking in pools
and low shrubs awaiting the approach of a suitable host, so as far
as angle of attack is concerned they have pretty much got it sewn
up. However, the ankle is particularly vulnerable and should be
well protected.

Colonel Godwin-Austen says: 'An effective way to prevent leeches
attacking the ankles and legs, is to wear woollen stockings; then over
them, round the legs, patawas, the woollen bandages as worn in the
Kashmir Himalaya, and now served out to our troops on mountain
service in India. Then, last, a pair of cotton socks tied above with

tape. After adopting this plan in the Terai and Assam I never got
bitten.

Hints to Travellers, 1883

* * *

Those who wish to shoot on the W. Coast should have gaiters steeped
in tobacco juice to keep off leeches.

Murray's Handbook for Bombay, 1881

In the same way that cigarette-smoking helps to keep public
houses mercifully free from puritans, young families and other
killjoys, it seems that tobacco products are equally efficacious in
keeping pests at bay abroad too.

Scorpions, Wasps and Bees

The benefits of tobacco usage do not end with its leech-repelling
qualities. As well as providing a good work-out for the bronchi-
oles, pipe smoking is recommended for those fearful of venomous insects such as scorpions and wasps. The aromatic fumes
produced by a pipe will deter insects from approaching and
simultaneously its bowl will brew up a handy remedy for the
treatment of stings.

For the stings of small scorpions [Fig. 5], wasps
etc., the oily residue scraped out of an old
tobacco pipe is said to be an effectual remedy.
Common stings of bees, etc., may generally be
almost instantaneously healed by applying a
handful of earth saturated in
vinegar.

*Murray's Handbook for
Travellers in Greece,*
1884

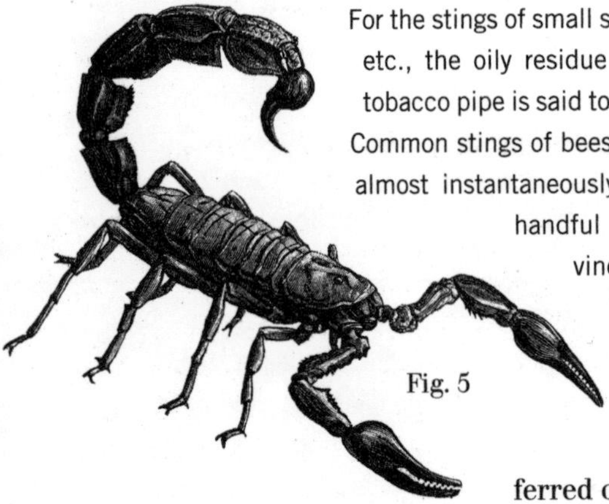

Fig. 5

Of course, the pre-
ferred object is not to get stung

in the first place. Whilst Mr Levinge's estimable device is all well and good during the night or when at rest, it is of precious little use during daylight hours when you have places to go and people to see. This is why ladies and gentlemen on the move must always ensure they are adequately protected by appropriate dress.

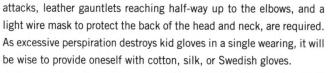

Fig. 6

> Spectacles, of a neutral tint, and a
> veil to protect the eyes from dust and from
> the attack of bees, are also very neces-
> sary. These troublesome insects have
> caused severe injuries and even death
> to travellers. To be quite safe from their
> attacks, leather gauntlets reaching half-way up to the elbows, and a
> light wire mask to protect the back of the head and neck, are required.
> As excessive perspiration destroys kid gloves in a single wearing, it will
> be wise to provide oneself with cotton, silk, or Swedish gloves.
>
> *Murray's Handbook for Bombay*, 1881

The attractive bee-retardant day suit shown in Fig. 6 proves that safety clothing need not look frumpy in order to be effective.

Snakes and Other Dangerous Creatures

Any journey of exploration is bound to involve a great deal of wading through waist-high rivers, swamps or tropical marsh-lands or pushing one's way through lush undergrowth, all of which can be the habitat of dangerous creatures. Snakes are par-ticularly clever at blending with their environment and although they tend to flee from animals as large as a human being, they will not take too kindly if you inadvertently tweak their tail with a size 13 hiking boot. If you do get bitten it is hoped that your

Fig. 7   *Tricky customers to deal with, snakes, like disgruntled workers, have a tendency to strike when you are least expecting it*

companions are not the squeamish type, but keen to attempt some small measure of amateur heroics that will earn them a brief mention in the *Basankusu Missionary Times* or some other publication of repute.

> Snake poison is 'dead' poison, and you can suck the wound if you rinse out your mouth with an antiseptic afterwards.
>
> *The Happy Traveller*, Revd Frank Tatchell, 1923

In less remote regions, and especially if you are not adequately equipped with a bottle of fifteen-year-old single malt antiseptic, then it is probably advisable not to hog the limelight but to allow local peasants to earn themselves a little glory instead.

> Travellers in Greece and the Archipelago (Rhodes and Cyprus excepted) are seldom troubled by noxious reptiles; still, as such exist, a word on the subject may be desirable. A faint odour of musk in the air is often a sign of their vicinity. If bitten by a snake or a scorpion, bind a handkerchief or string firmly above the injured part, to prevent the poison spreading in the blood. Do not trust of amateur surgery, but get medical advice as speedily as possible. Failing this, there is generally some old peasant to be found capable of treating such cases. Above all, do not yield to lethargy or drowsiness which is the common result of snake bite, and often ends fatally.
>
> *Murray's Handbook for Travellers in Greece*, 1884

Adequate recompense should be offered to any old peasant for providing such services. For advice on appropriate tipping refer to Chapter 8; generally speaking, for saving one's life by sucking poison out of a wound, the gift of a rather nice biro or a small plastic thimble is thought to be more than adequate.

Slightly more difficult customers to deal with are piranhas. Stories abound about the voracity and aggression of these little blighters, and many are simply untrue. Rumour has it that when conditions are right, an attack can happen so fast that one has no idea that one is actually being bitten. Clearly some myths need to

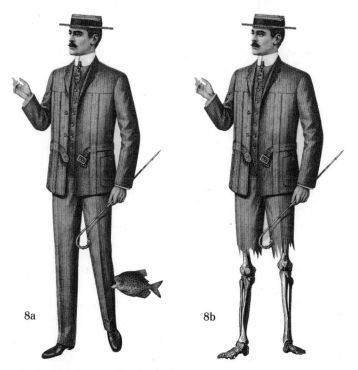

8a   8b

Fig. 8   *The danger from piranhas is often greatly exaggerated. The classic symptoms of attack are shown in Fig. 8a. If you exhibit the characteristics shown in Fig. 8b the cause is far more likely to be having gone paddling inadvisably close to the outfall of a corrosive chemical plant*

be dispelled. If in doubt, Fig. 8 shows symptoms you should look out for.

Hygiene and Exercise

Exercise

Exercise other than a brisk stroll is an extremely over-rated activity. The traveller will soon realise that the mere act of exploring is strenuous enough in itself without indulging in artificial forms of exertion. At home, he may be bamboozled by glossy magazines into signing up with a gymnasium or making an utter idiot of himself by running around the park in his underwear; in the tropics, conditions will thankfully militate against indulging in vigorous exercise.

> It is hardly necessary to urge the injuriousness of every kind of active exercises to Europeans under tropical heats, and especially the heats of the day, yet hundreds perish annually from this very cause.
>
> *The Influence of Tropical Climates on European Constitutions*,
> James Ranald Martin, 1855

Other far more pleasant means of keeping the system in fine fettle will be discovered.

> The languid state of the circulation of the blood in old Indians is pointedly shewn in the disposition to raise the lower extremities on a line with the body when at rest . . . On the same principal may be explained the pleasurable feeling and utility of shampooing, where the gentle pressure and friction of the soft Asiatic hand over the surface of the body, but particularly over the limbs, invigorate the circulation after fatigue, as well as after long inaction, and excite the inert circular secretion. The kisa or hair-glove of India is an admirable means of giving additional effect to shampooing, a practice which to the indolent wealthy natives is a real and effective substitute for exercise.
>
> *Murray's Handbook for India*, 1859

Mrs Darkwood was always most insistent on having her inert circular secretion excited every Friday night during our sojourn in India. She would keep Nandi, our glove boy, occupied for up to two hours at a time, and emerged from her room quite aglow and brimming with health. So much so, in fact, that I was rather tempted to try it for myself, but unfortunately Nandi, poor fellow, put so much dedication into these shampooing sessions that he would rarely have the energy to do me the same service afterwards. One must not complain: it is a rare event, and always gratifying, to witness a servant fulfilling his duties to the very maximum.

The only other permissible form of exertion in a tropical climate is dancing. Indulging in a light foxtrot or a waltz will usually do no harm, but on particularly oppressive days anything more strenuous should remain a spectator sport.

> Who would expect to find dancing a prominent amusement in a tropical climate? The natives of the West Indies are exceedingly fond of this exercise; but those of the East are wise men still, for instead of dancing themselves they employ Natch girls to dance for them.
>
> *The Influence of Tropical Climates on European Constitutions*,
> James Ranald Martin, 1855

Bathing

In the filthy heat of the Tropics nothing is more tempting than to fling oneself into a daily bath of iced water, but the shock to the system produced by such foolhardiness can result in mischief.

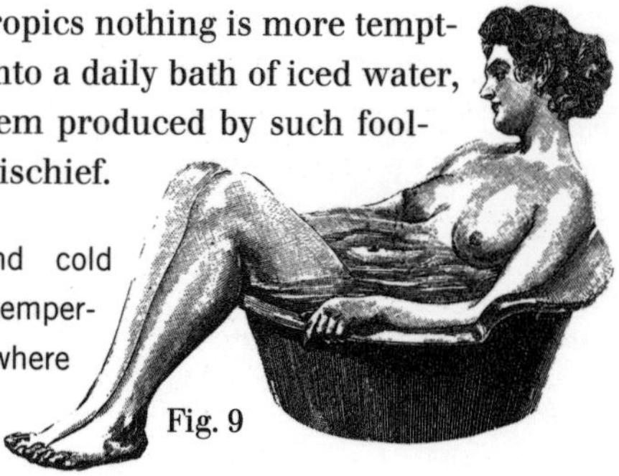

Fig. 9

> I DARE not recommend cold bathing; it is death with intemperance, and dangerous where there is any fault with the viscera. It is a luxury

177

denied to almost all, except the sober and abstemious females, who well know the delights and advantages of it [Fig.9].

Dr Moseley in The Influence of Tropical Climates on European Constitutions, James Ranald Martin, 1855

For inebriate males alternative methods of maintaining hygiene will have to be found. In his book *Half-Cut in Calcutta* renowned old soak Major-General Felix Gaughstley-Whynne swears by being hosed down every morning with the assistance of his mahout and a specially trained elephant, but such specialised techniques, whilst effective, may not be convenient for general use. Alternatively, a servant with a jug of water may work just as well.

If cold water be used it should be quickly poured over the body, which should be rapidly and thoroughly dried by strong friction with rough towels . . . After bathing or wading in the waters of tropical countries the skin should be thoroughly dried, care being taken to remove all moisture from depressions where it may escape the action of the towel, otherwise an opportunity for lodgement is afforded to the numerous vegetable and animal parasites that infest such waters.

Hints to Travellers, 1883

* * *

To put the feet into warm water for a couple of minutes before going to bed is very refreshing and inviting to sleep: for promoting tranquillity, both mental and corporeal, a clean skin may be regarded as next in efficacy as a clear conscience.

The Traveller's Oracle, Dr William Kitchiner, 1827

Whichever method you adopt, the brisk rub-down with a rough towel is absolutely essential for the Englishman who wishes to prevent the development conditions such as *lascivium chronicus* and 'inflammation of the dander' that are all too likely to occur in hot climates. For guidance on the conduct and government of the passions see the relevant section in Chapter 13.

CHAPTER THE ELEVENTH

Advocating a Code of Conduct for

THE
ENGLISHMAN
ABROAD

THE ENGLISHMAN ABROAD

It is tempting when planning a journey to regard the whole process as a purely technical undertaking. The traveller can all too easily spend all of his time attending to practical matters – calculating the precise poundage of luggage to be carried by each animal; the distance to be covered per day; the exact ratio of bottles of gin to those of vermouth that ought to be packed. One should never regard a foreign land as merely a museum, or a piece of topography, or a natural resource that needs to be explored, surveyed or exploited. With luck it may be all three, but one should not lose sight of the fact,

Fig. 1

inconvenient though it may be, that ninety-nine times out of a hundred the country you are visiting is also likely to be home to an indigenous population (e.g., Fig. 1). If you harbour any plans to carve up their country into easily manageable chunks, set up a noxious chemical plant or two, and export a few of their surplus art treasures, this will be made a lot easier if you get on with the locals like a house on fire. (This is always preferable to Plan B, which is actually to set their houses on fire.)

Winning Friends and Influencing People

Just because an Englishman may be reasonably affluent compared to some of his overseas cousins, this does not give him the right to treat everyone he meets as minions (unless, that is, they have been employed in that particular capacity). Luckily, such lamentable attitudes are usually restricted to the ranks of the *nouveaux riches* such as estate agents, persons of trade, dot-com millionaires and the like. The true English gentleman is always careful to bring a little *noblesse oblige* to the fore.

> It is a fact deeply to be regretted that many vulgar and half-witted Englishmen think, if they leave home with money they can command anything; that it is mean to be civil, and beneath them to feel grateful for any efforts to oblige them made by those for whose services they pay. The presumption of our countrymen is proverbial on the Continent, fortunately, the exceptions are numerous, and we are spoken of as an unaccountable people, when some men of unquestionable character and fortune display examples of suavity and true gentility which cannot be surpassed on earth; the foreigner is thus puzzled to know how to estimate our national character.
>
> *Murray's Handbook for Travellers in Denmark, Norway, Sweden, and Iceland*, 1858

* * *

> Do not forget that foreigners will form their idea of Englishmen from the way you act; so always be jealous for England's honour and always play the game. Few things are more distressing to an honest traveller than to see the bad behaviour of some of his countrymen abroad. To talk loudly in the streets and cafés, to walk about the cathedrals during mass and generally to ignore the rules of politeness is not the way to make the English well liked in foreign countries. The Germans are the worst offenders, having, in addition to these failings, a grossness in their way of eating and a gloating zeal in collecting salacious post cards, but some English folk are almost as bad.
>
> *The Happy Traveller*, Revd Frank Tatchell, 1923

Adopting an open and interested demeanour and artfully feigning an appreciation of your hosts' culture can win over hearts and minds in a trice.

Instead of finding fault with the customs of a place, and telling the people that the English ones are a thousand times better (as my countrymen are apt to do), commend their table, their dress, their houses, and their manners, a little more, it may be, than you really think they deserve: this degree of complaisance is neither criminal nor abject; it is but a small price to pay for the good-will and affection of the people you converse with. As the generality of people are weak enough to be pleased with these little things, those who refuse to please them so cheaply are weaker than they.

The Traveller's Oracle, Dr William Kitchiner, 1827

We have already seen how spreading a few baubles and trinkets about the place will put one on a favourable footing with the local peasantry, but when meeting with equals one is more likely to be able to curry favour by introducing some dignified practices from back home. With snuff lovers, hand around a burgeoning box of Brunswick Black Rappee; or with younger, sporty types, challenge them to a playful duel – always a marvellous method of bonding with local men of valour. For the more sedate, the following may be of use.

Carry many visiting cards; foreigners delight in exchanging them, and they are useful in the East for leaving at the local club, where you will no doubt be made an honorary member for the duration of your stay [Fig. 2].

The Happy Traveller, Revd Frank Tatchell, 1923

Fig. 2

National Character

Whilst people across the globe hold many characteristics in common, it is well to temper one's enthusiasm for the *oneness of man*, by making due allowance for quirks of national character. To some, the singling out of these differences may seem racially prejudiced, but surely it is far more arrogant to expect, for example, a Frenchman to conform to our own standards of oral hygiene than for us to accept, with a resigned shrug, that his ways may be very different from our own. Forewarned is forearmed – so here, by way of an introduction, are a few helpful observations made by experienced travellers.

The Malays have clean bodies but dirty houses, in spite of the fact that a man is allowed four wives. They are the greatest loafers on the face of the earth and will not work for themselves or anyone else.

The Happy Traveller, Revd Frank Tatchell, 1923

* * *

The Dutch are generally tall, strong built people; but both men and women have the grossest shapes that are to be met with anywhere or rather no shape at all. Their motion is as disagreeable as their shape, being very heavy and awkward, insomuch that 'tis an easy matter to distinguish a Dutchman from a native of England or France, almost the length of a street, by his mien.

The Grand Tour, Thomas Nugent, 1749

* * *

The Swiss people generally 'are the Dutch of the mountains; the same cold, unimaginative, money-seeking, yet vigorous, determined, ener-getic people, at the head of the moral state in Europe for honesty, fidelity to their engagements, sobriety, industry, good government, general well-being – yet at the bottom of the scale for religious feel-ings, observances, and knowledge.' – Notes of a Traveller.

Longman's Practical Swiss Guide, 1856

* * *

Nothing is more common among the Germans than to form drinking societies, where they contract an intimacy by being drunk together.

Their excess in drinking is accompanied with intemperance in eating; no people indulge their bellies more than the inhabitants of this country.

The Grand Tour, Thomas Nugent, 1749

* * *

Italian driving is a little peculiar. It consists in walking in the wide roads, and driving furiously in the narrow streets; so that pedestrians are in continual danger of having their toes amputated. Many of the streets of Florence have the look of immense laundries, every window being turned into a drying ground; and scarecrow legs tied one to another dangling in the air, and flapping about in the wind. The sheets, the bedding, continually may be seen out 'airing'. The washing in Italy is a great mystery, a sort of eternal penance – forever washing, yet never clean.

Going Abroad, Nona Bellairs, 1857

* * *

Never forget that the Spaniard is of a very high caste and a gentle-man by innate aristocracy; proud as Lucifer and combustible as his matches, he is punctilious and touchy on the point of honour [e.g., Fig. 3].

Murray's Handbook for Travellers in Spain, 1847

With these differences duly noted, the explorer is now in a good position from which to engage meaningfully with his temporary hosts.

Modes of Salutation

When first meeting the indigenous population, unless you have a command of the local lingo, most communication will be through tone of voice, gesture and sign language. On first contact, the most useful of these will be some recognisable form of salutation. If in doubt, a firm handshake accompanied by a brisk 'A very good day

to you' usually does the trick. Alternatively, if your reception com-
mittee is carrying spears, cudgels or guns, it might be wise to
avoid thrusting your hand forward, and a slight nod or a gracious
bow may do just as well. Ideally, though, doing a little research
and employing the locally favoured custom is the best way to
dispel any initial awkwardness.

When men salute each other in an amicable manner, it signifies little
whether they move a particular part of the body, or practice a particular ceremony. Every nation imagines it employs the most reasonable
ones; but all are equally simple, and none are to be treated as
ridiculous.

The Islanders, near the Philippines, take the hand or foot of him
they salute, and with it they gently rub their face.

The Laplanders apply their nose strongly against that of the person
they salute.

Other salutations are very incommodious and painful; it requires
great practice to enable a man to be polite in an
island situated in the Streights of the Sound.

Fig. 3

[Cornelis] Houtman tells us, they saluted
him in this odd way: 'They raised his left
foot, which they passed gently over the
right leg, and from thence over his face.'

The inhabitants of the Philippines use
a most complex attitude; they bend their
body very low, place their hands on their
cheeks, and raise at the same time one foot
in the air with their knee bent.

Barbarous nations frequently imprint on
their salutations the dispositions of their character. When the inhabitants of Carmina (says
Athenaeus) would show a particular mark of
esteem, they breathed a vein, and presented
for the beverage of their friends the blood as it
issued.

> The Franks tore hair from the head, and presented it to those
> persons they saluted.
>
> *English Traditions and Foreign Customs*, George Laurence Gomme, 1885

I beg to differ from George Gomme's assertion that no forms of
salutation should be treated as ridiculous. If Mr Gomme is happy
to tear chunks of hair from his head and have guests use his face
as a doormat then that is no concern of mine, but I assure him
that they are practices that are highly unlikely to catch on in the
more fashionable quarters of Knightsbridge.

When it comes to sign language it is best to avoid any hand gestures that involve complex configurations of fingers unless you
know exactly what you are doing. The hand gesture that conveys
to a hotelier that he serves the best *gâteaux* in town in one country
may well be used to insinuate that his wife has slept with the best
part of the local football team in another. Misunderstandings of
this sort are notoriously difficult to iron out amicably.

Speaking the Language

Traditional wisdom has it that if you bellow English at the top of
your lungs whilst maintaining eye contact with a foreigner, he is
bound to understand every word you say. In my experience, I have
rarely found this to be the case. Even though Englishmen are piti-
fully inept at mastering other peoples' languages, they should at
least make some effort to acquire a smattering of the local *patois*.
Even if his mastery amounts to no more than a handful of individual words and the phrase for 'Excuse me, is this the cheese
counter?', then it is only politeness to attempt to weave these
into the conversation wherever he can. Delivering these words
with the kindly intonation that a nurse uses when speaking
to an elderly patient, a traveller will be surprised how easily
he can make himself understood.

> Chat with everyone you meet and if a native does not understand you,
> do not shout or try to put it another way, since that will only confuse

him all the more; and, especially, keep grave face when a foreigner talks atrocious English to you.

The Happy Traveller, Revd Frank Tatchell, 1923

In the end, it is in a traveller's own interests to master at least a rough understanding of his host's language.

The common people, in every country, understand only their native tongue; and as a traveller must necessarily make use of them as land-lords, postilions, tradesmen, &c., you may easily imagine, that a traveller will be liable to numerous insults and impositions if he is ignorant of their language.

The Traveller's Oracle, Dr William Kitchiner, 1827

Some servants simply will not respond to your commands unless you couch them in terms they understand.

When talking to your Chinese 'boy' [Fig. 4] you use Pidgin English. This is a corruption of business English; thus, when he says that something is not his 'pidgin', he means that it is outside his particular work, which no true Chinaman will overstep by a hair's breadth.

Here are a few of the words used and their meanings: Chop chop, quickly; all same this, like this ; can do, I will; no can do, I won't; fie tee, hurry; man man, stop; how fashion, how much? no can cuttee, cheaper; no b'long plopper, that won't do; one piecee, one thing; number one, best; maski, all right or never mind. Though round about, this baby mode of talk is tolerably successful. No one has

Fig. 4

taught him to use the word 'Bishop' but his own 'topside joss pidgin fellow' expresses both the idea and the dignity.

The Happy Traveller, Revd Frank Tatchell, 1923

To my ear, this certainly has a very pleasant ring to it. In fact, I have written to the General Synod recently to suggest adoption of this form of address by the Church of England. The election of the first Topside Joss Pidgin Fellow of Bath and Wells can surely be only a matter of time.

If mastering outlandish foreign tongues is not your forté it might be wise to invest in a set of Levington-Trussett pictogram cards. Available in packs of forty, they are indispensible in situations where communcation is vital, but you have little idea of local language or custom. Each card bears a simple pictograph designed to be universally understood across the globe (Fig. 5).

More champagne, please.

I am displeased.

I am very displeased.

Are your beds clean?

We wish to build a railway through your village

You are now a subject of Her Majesty the Queen

Fig. 5 *Examples from the Levington-Trussett System of international pictographic communication*

❄

The Englishman Abroad

50 Indispensible Foreign Phrases

For braver souls who do not mind having a bash at the local argot the following sentences have been scientifically compiled as a lexicon of the fifty most outstandingly useful phrases for the world traveller. They have been selected from various hand-books and conversation guides including: *Baedeker's Travellers Manual of Conversation in four languages,* 1886; *A Handbook of the Swahili Language,* 1918 and *Chinese without a Teacher: Easy and Useful Sentences in the Mandarin Dialect,* 1872.

Spanish

You are a pretty jewel.
Buena alhaja, buena prenda es Vind.

He is very ugly.
Tiene cara de hereje.

She is very scraggy.
Tiene pecho como tabla de animas.

I am suffocated with rage.
Vengo sofocado.

Little Conchita has a wicked tongue.
Mala lengua tiene Conchita.

Russian

Where is my servant?
Gdé moi chelovék?

I will not give you any drink money.
Nedàm na vòdku.

Panjábi

Torch-bearer, run a little before me.
Masálchiá, mere muhre chall.

Has any sick person slept on this bed lately?
Ki ajj kath koi roggi is wich-háuñe pur suttá hai?

Have done with your smoking and go on.
Hukke nún chhaddo ate chale challo.

Hindi

Pour it over me from the leather bag.

Masak se dálo hamáre upar.

Find my slippers.
Silpat talásh karo.

Don't bring cow's milk, but buffalo's milk.
Gaé ke dúdh mat lúo bhains ke dúdh láo.

Japanese

What a horrid smell.
Kusai! Kusai!

Please engage two coolies.
Ninsoku futari tanonde kuda-sai.

Swedish

Call us at seven to-morrow morning, and let the horses be ready by eight.
Väck oss klockan sju i morgan bittida, och låt hüstorne vara järdiga klockan åtta.

German

If you do everything to my satisfaction, I will reward you liberally.
Wenn Sie Alles zu meiner Zufriedenheit besorgen, werde ich Sie gut belohnen.

Do not drive so near to that precipice.
Fahrt nicht so nahe an diesem Abgrund.

I want my bed warmed directly.
Ich wünsche mein Bett gleich gewärmt zu haben.

I cannot bear much more of that; please be gentle.
Diesen Schmerz kann ich nicht mehr erdulden; bitte, seien Sie vorsichtig.

Have you fresh leeches? These do not bite.
Haben Sie frische Bluegel? Diese beissen nicht an.

French

Would you oblige me, Sir, by not humming?
Voudriez-vous avoir la bonté, Monsieur, de ne pas fredonner?

I am to take twenty-one baths; please give me a ticket for that number.
J'ai vingt-un bains à prendre; veuillez m'en donner les billets!

Are the postillions insolent?
Les postillions sont-ils insolents?

Smell some eau de Cologne, it will do you good.
Respirez un peu d'eau de Cologne, cela vous fera du bien.

I killed it myself the day before yesterday.
C'est moi qui l'ai tuée avant-hier.

I have had a slight attack of the gout, which has forced me to keep my room for a fortnight.
J'ai en un léger accès de goutte, qui m'a obligé de garder la chambre pendant quinze jours.

Italian

Do you like turbot, Sir?
Le piace il rombo?

I think that soup weakens the stomach.
Credo che la zuppa indebolisca lo stomacho.

I shall be very well placed here opposite the Countess.
Io starò benissimo qui, in faccia alla signora contessa.

A short conversation with one's tailor:
Customer: I will first try on my nankeen pantaloons, and afterwards my trowsers and coat.
C: Voglio provare prima di tutto i pantaloni di nauchina, poi proverò gli altri pantaloni ed il vestito.

After trying them on . . .

C: These pantaloons are too tight and too short.
C: Questi pantaloni sono troppo stretti e troppo corti.

Tailor: They are not worn now so wide and so long, as they were a fortnight ago.
T: Non si portano più, signore, nè così larghi, nè così lunghi, come si portavano quindici giorno fa.

C: Is fashion changed already?
C: Come! è già cambiata la moda?

T: It changes every week, Sir.
T: Signore, ella cambia tutte le settimane.

Portuguese

Bring me a foot bath, some hot wine and water.

Traga-me um banho para os pés, uma sangria.

You must forgive me if I am not intelligible.
Queira desculpar-me se me não faço entender.

If you do it again, I shall complain to your master.
Se fizer outra vez, farei queixa ao seu amo.

I want a rice pudding.
Quero um pudim de arroz.

Will you do me the honour to dance the next waltz with me?
Quer V.E. fazer me a honra de dançar comigo a primiera valsa?

A mustard poltice to be placed on the chest at once.
Ponhe já uma cataplasma de mostardo no pieto.

Swahili

When you have swept the room put on clean clothes.
Kamma umekwisha kufagia, vaa nguo safi.

I am never without pimples.
Vipele havinitoka kabisa.
The baobabs are now coming into leaf.
Siku hizi mibuyu inachanua majani.

If he strikes you, hit him again.
Akikupiga, nawe impiga tena.

Chinese

My wife is dead.
Woaty foo-ren sirla.

I must give you a thrashing.
Woa yow tah nee.

You are a bad man.
Nee pooshirt how ren.

I want to take off my clothes.
Woa yow t'oa eeshahng.

This telescope is mine.
Chayka ch'e-enleeyenn shirt woaty.

CHAPTER THE TWELFTH

Assisting the Traveller to Deal with

HOSTILITIES
AND PERSONAL
SECURITY

HOSTILITIES AND PERSONAL SECURITY

Avoiding Trouble

Journeying the high-
ways and byways of
far-off lands, the traveller will
naturally encounter numerous
hirsute and swarthy types untutored
in an Englishman's genteel graces and
codes of etiquette; but merely because a
foreigner may exhibit lamentable standards of personal hygiene, possesses but
three teeth in his head and be rough-hewn
in manners, it is unjust to conclude that he
will also be untrustworthy, larcenous and
intent upon doing one physical harm.
He may very well be all of these
things, but an innate sense of justice
will compel one, initially at least, to
give him the benefit of the doubt:

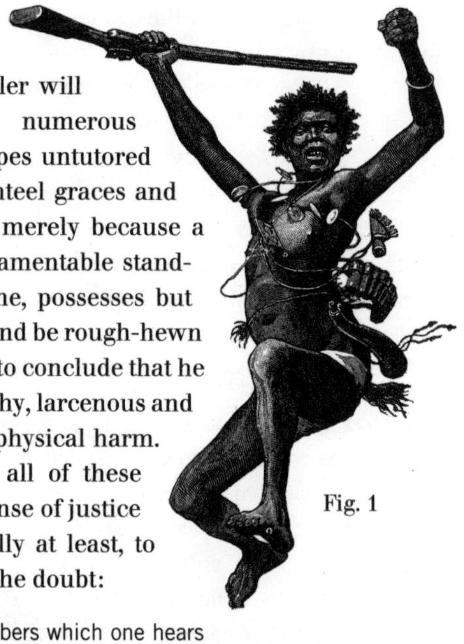

Fig. 1

Many of the tales of robbers which one hears
abroad are invented by guides who resent that a man should go about
alone; and a traveller soon finds out that a peasant with every mark
of being a brigand may be a very peaceable person. His wild appearance is probably due to you seeing him at the wrong end of the week
because, on the Continent, poor men only get shaved on Saturday. If
you do really meet a 'suspicious character' in a lonely place, do not

hesitate but keep on with an added jauntiness; and do not go round,
which would argue that you are afraid, but rather steer more directly
for him. If you like you can finger an imaginary revolver in your hip
pocket, but a cheery and confident good-day is usually enough. Do
not look back.

The Happy Traveller, Revd Frank Tatchell, 1923

Naturally, it is sensible to avoid placing oneself in a situation that
might lead to conflict in the first place. Walking down poorly lit
thoroughfares, drunkenly discussing the idiocy of the national
religion in a crowded bar, or looking at locals in a funny way
should be avoided if at all possible. Sometimes, though, through
no fault of one's own, it becomes obvious that confrontation is
inevitable. If you sense that some form of nastiness is about to
unfold, you should try various methods of defusing the situation
to avoid being forced into a bout of fisticuffs or some other
unpleasantness. These will include Tatchell's 'added
jauntiness', strategic retreat (running away) and, if all
else fails, a spot of unabashed pleading coupled with
the proffering of items of personal jewellery and hard
cash.

How to Treat Banditti – Should the traveller have the
misfortune to fall into the hands of bandits, he
ought to be prepared with a sufficient sum about
his person, say from £5 to £10, in order to keep
the riflers in good humour, as they
are prone to make an example of
the unfortunate individual who
evinces, by empty pockets, the
malice prepense of depriving
them of what they consider their
just perquisites; in such a case
they will inflict blows and other
chastisement, strip the body, and
leave it half dead. A common gilt

Fig. 2

watch and chain [Fig. 2] ought not to be omitted. Travellers, except when well armed and forming a large party, should not resist a regular band of robbers, as it is seldom of any avail, and will frequently lead to fatal consequences; the best plan is to make a frank good-humoured surrender; presence of mind and a calm courteous appeal to them as Caballeros seldom fails to conciliate them, and moderate their outrages. It is better to lose one's money than one's life, and to submit with a good grace to the polite request of putting your mouth downwards, into the mud.

Hardships in Travel Made Easy, 1864

There is no shame in capitulation under such circumstances. Even so, as I know from my own experience, there will always be some member of your party who feels it is incumbent upon them to question your tactics. Mrs Darkwood, for example, once insinuated that the act of throwing myself onto my knees, sobbing loudly and begging for mercy when confronted by a band of brigands in Chile could possibly be construed as cowardice. Elaborate military ploys of this kind may indeed be misinterpreted by the untrained eye of the civilian, until it is pointed out to them that such strategies are merely designed to divert attention away from the weaker members of the group. It is a sad fact that the skilled tactician often has to put up with the feeble-minded carpings of underlings ignorant of the subtleties of psychological warfare.

Repelling Hostilities

Sadly, despite one's best endeavours at peacemaking, events can sometimes take a turn for the worse, and you could find yourself embroiled in a fracas with people who neither speak your language nor have much regard for Western rules of chivalry or engagement. At times like these a traveller must fall back on his own mettle and improvise with whatever may come to hand.

Fig. 3

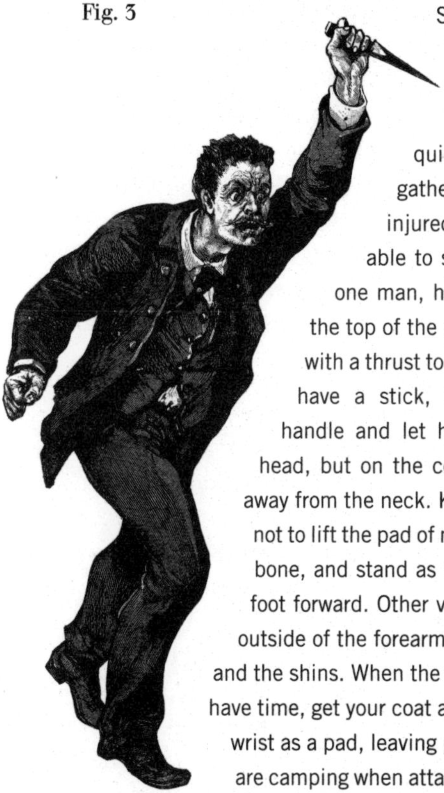

Should you be attacked by a mob in the East, hurt one of the crowd and hurt him quickly. The others will gather chattering round the injured man and you will be able to slip away. If attacked by one man, hold your umbrella round the top of the ribs and meet his charge with a thrust to the belly or throat. If you have a stick, hold it just below the handle and let him have it, not on the head, but on the collar-bone an inch or so away from the neck. Keep your hand low so as not to lift the pad of muscle behind the collar-bone, and stand as in fencing with the right foot forward. Other vulnerable places are the outside of the forearm, the tip of the shoulder, and the shins. When the man has a knife and you have time, get your coat and wrap it round the left wrist as a pad, leaving part of it dangling. If you are camping when attacked, leap away from the fire into the dark and keep still. To catch the faintest sound, keep your mouth open, for our ear has an inward entrance as well as an outer, like the gill which gave it origin. If you have a companion and want to wake him without his speaking, press with your finger under his ear.

The Happy Traveller, Revd Frank Tatchell, 1923

Apart from flashes of ingenuity with a brolly, other effective methods of self-defence include such classics as a poke in the eye, stamping on the foot, or running the serrated edge of a comb along the underside of an assailant's nose. All three of these must be done with certainty and vigour, otherwise they will only serve to exacerbate matters, and you will merely find yourself grappling with an opponent who is doubly enraged, albeit blind in one eye and hopping.

Other advice often given to travellers concerned about their safety is that they should learn some form of martial art such as Aikido or Tae Kwon Do, but in my experience, unless one becomes a complete expert in such techniques, they can be more of a hindrance than a blessing. The valuable seconds spent trying to recall the precise method recommended for repelling a mob in the East, for example, could be better employed merely making a run for it. The only glimmer of hope for a novice attempting to practise his art is that the very sight of him adopting the pose of the coiled cobra is likely to reduce his assailants to a state of helpless mirth, therefore enabling him to make good his escape.

Security Precautions

With some forethought the traveller can avoid both capitulation and engagement by taking sensible security precautions designed to prevent things 'kicking off' in the first place. One of the most reliable methods for deterring potential molesters is to equip oneself with an impressive array of firearms.

In many cases it is absolutely necessary that the traveller should be well armed, in order to resist attempts which may be made upon his life; the simple fact of his being thus prepared, accompanied by showing a bold front and a determination not to yield, will frequently be sufficient to stay any further proceedings on the part of

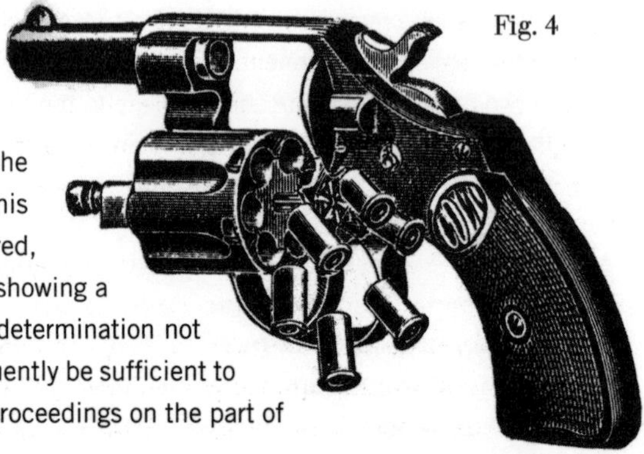

Fig. 4

those who are about to molest him. One of Colt's revolvers is the best implement in the shape of fire-arms [Fig. 4], and if properly handled will do most deadly execution on a very short space of time. A dirk fitted into a sheath at the side, and a life-preserver for the pocket, complete the weapons of defence for the traveller's purpose. Attacks upon the person, however, are not confined to the hours when a person is abroad; the time of sleep is sometimes selected, and the unfortunate traveller set upon when he is least able to defend himself.

Hardships in Travel Made Easy, 1864

Indeed, even in the supposedly secure environment of a hotel room it is advisable to take nothing for granted.

Pocket door bolts, which are applicable to almost all sorts of doors, may on many occasions save the property and the life of the traveller: it is advisable to be always provided with such bolts. The corkscrew door-fastening is the simplest that we have seen; this is screwed in between the door and the door-post, and unites them so firmly, that great power is required to force a door so fastened. They are as portable as common corkscrews, and their weight does not exceed an ounce and a half.

The safety of your bedroom door should always be carefully examined; and in case of bolts not being at hand, it will be useful to hinder entrance into the room, by putting a table and chair upon it against the door; such precautions are, however, less necessary in England than they are on the Continent, where it is advisable to choose a room with two beds, and let your servant sleep in the room, and to burn a light all night: when you enter the room to go to rest, take a peep behind and under the beds, closets, &c. and all places where concealment is possible.

The Traveller's Oracle, Dr William Kitchiner, 1827

Stourbridge, my trusty batman, exhibits fantastic stamina in his duties as night watchman. He will selflessly volunteer to sit up all night on guard over Mrs Darkwood, allowing me to gain a good night's repose in my own highly-fortified chamber. I was once awoken by a frightful row emanating from my wife's room, consisting of a series of bumps and crashes, only to find on investigating that an intruder had tried to gain access through the window of the room with the intent of ravishing my wife. By the time I arrived the interloper had already escaped into the night, but by the look of things there had been quite a struggle – bed clothes and furniture everywhere. Thank heavens for Stourbridge. I have no idea what I would do without him.

On the whole, risk of assault is comparatively greater when outside one's bedchamber. Abroad, scoundrels are apt to lurk in every roadside thicket, but do not be surprised if you also find them lurking behind the reception desk of the wayside inn you are planning to check in to.

> In lonesome places, where an accident may oblige you to rest, if you carry fire arms, it may be well to let the landlord see (as it were accidentally) that you are well armed.
>
> *The Traveller's Oracle*, Dr William Kitchiner, 1827

But statistically the open road is where a traveller is most vulnerable and he should at all times advertise his intention not to be meddled with.

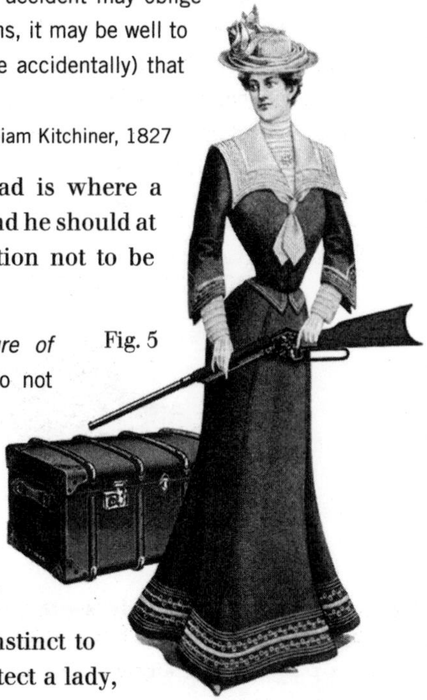

> Mr La Combe, in his *Picture of London*, advises those who do not wish to be robbed, to carry a brace of blunderbusses, and to put the muzzle of one out of each window, so as to be seen by the robbers!!!
>
> *The Gentleman's Magazine*, 1795

Fig. 5

It is a gentleman's natural instinct to put his life on the line to protect a lady, but in these times, when women are 'doing it for themselves', it should not be ruled out that she may wish to handle firearms of her own, and be perfectly capable of doing so.

Every lady should, to my mind, know how to use a revolver. She may at any time be in China or some other country where there are savage natives; and there is none of that danger of bruising the body, which is so harmful to ladies using guns or rifles.

Hints on Revolver Shooting, Walter Winans, 1904

My recommendation of a suitable firearm for a lady is a petite pearl-handled Deringer (Fig. 6) secreted in a sequinned clutch bag, but, as luck would have it, ladies are spoilt for choice when it comes to selecting a resting place for a pistol.

A lady can carry a revolver hidden for self-defence in many more ways than a man, owing to her draperies affording more places for concealment. Cloaks, capes, etc., make good hiding places for a revolver; inside a muff is about one of the best places; and a small revolver in the right hand, inside a muff, that hand hanging down by the side, is ready for instant use. As ladies often carry their muffs in this way, it does not arouse suspicion.

Hints on Revolver Shooting, Walter Winans, 1904

COLT'S "DERINGER" PISTOL.

Fig. 6

To carry in Waistcoat Pocket, &c., takes the ·410 Cartridge rim fire.
2½ in. barrel ; weight, 8 oz. ; total length, 4⅞ in. £0 16 0

An efficient and most portable Pistol.

Engaging in a Gun Battle

The real fun of hostilities only starts when a traveller is able to engage the enemy in a gun battle, but opening fire is a course of action that should always be kept as a last resort. Only in exceptional circumstances is it permissible to fire the opening shot. If you are threatened with imminent death; if it happens to be the fifth time you've been held up that afternoon; or if your assailants make snidey remarks about cricket or Her Majesty the Queen: then you have every right to make a pre-emptive strike.

> For a case where you are likely to be robbed, the inside breast pocket (where bank-notes are usually carried) is a good place for the revolver, as, when you are asked for your money, you can appear to be taking it out of this pocket whilst you are really drawing the revolver; or the revolver can be shot from this pocket without drawing it . . . Shooting through the pocket is as quick and unexpected a way as any; another is to turn partly away, and in doing so draw and fire from behind your back, or under your other arm.
>
> *Hints on Revolver Shooting*, Walter Winans, 1904

The annoying thing with gun battles is that one's opponent has a tendency to get riled and start shooting back willy-nilly with little thought for health and safety. As the situation escalates, you can take a little time to get your breath back by darting behind walls, sofas and, outdoors, items of street furniture.

> Out of doors, too, a lamp-post, or other narrow object, will spoil a man's aim by making him try to hit that part of you which shows on either side instead of his having your full width to aim at, even if it is too narrow or small fully to protect you [Fig. 7]. It is better not to try to give him a small mark to aim at by standing sideways, as then, if he hits you, he will rake all through your vitals; whereas, if you are facing him squarely, he may put several bullets into you without fatal effects.
>
> *Hints on Revolver Shooting*, Walter Winans, 1904

After half an hour or so of throwing chairs, ducking and diving, and leaping out of windows etc., there comes a moment in any gun battle where opponents accidentally bump into each other whilst turning a corner, and have to engage in a close-up tussle. This will result in some very cinematic grappling: pistols scudding across the floor, guns sitting tantalisingly an inch or two out of reach, each of you taking turns to have the upper hand. This is the ideal time to try and disable your assailant.

> If a man does not look desperate and capable of continuing shooting till he is killed, if you can break his shooting wrist it may be sufficient, and if he should try to shift his pistol from the disabled hand to the other, you can break that also.
>
> *Hints on Revolver Shooting*, Walter Winans, 1904

Reduced to a cripple, an enemy can be safely taken into custody.

Fig. 7 *Adopting cunning methods of concealment can render the shootist virtually invisible to the untrained eye*

Taking Prisoners

All confrontations have repercussions that may result in the involvement of the local law enforcement agencies and judicial system. If you have been assailed far from local habitation and you have only injured or captured your opponent, it will be your responsibility to deliver the fellow into the hands of the proper authorities. If the nearest town is several days'

journey away it is impor-
tant to secure your pris-
oner before transporting
him.

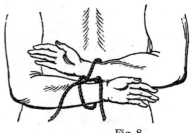

Fig. 8

Tying the hands – To tie a
man's hands behind his
back, take a handkerchief,
it is the best thing; failing
that, a thin cord. It is necessary that its length should not be less than
2 feet, but 2 feet 6 inches is the right length; for a double tie, it
should be 3 feet 6 inches. Compel him to lay his hands as in the
sketch [Fig. 8], and, wrapping the cord once (or twice if it be long
enough) round the arms, pretty lightly, pass the longest end in
between the arms as shown in the figure, and tie quite tightly. If you
are quick in tying the common 'tom-fool's knots', well known to every
sailor, it is still better for the purpose. Put the prisoner's hands one
within each loop, then draw tightly the running ends, and knot them
together.

   Tying the Thumbs – To secure a prisoner with the least amount of
string, place his hands back to back, behind him, then tie the
thumbs together, and also the little fingers. Two bits of thin string,
each a foot long, will thoroughly do this, But, if you have not any
string at hand, cut a thong from his leather apron, or tear a strip from
your own linen.

The Art of Travel, Francis Galton, 1872

A further method of securing a prisoner is one that I discovered
recently whilst sorting through some loose illustrations.
Known as La Changa (Figs. 9a & 9b) it is a device that appears
to be slightly more cumbersome than handcuffs and therefore
a little tricky to pack, but it does have one advantage – it can be
swiftly fashioned from a requisitioned garden gate. It is worth
keeping as an option if you unexpectedly acquire a prisoner
along the way, and find yourself fresh out of string or sturdy
twine.

Figs. 9a & 9b *La Changa is a highly effective way of securing a prisoner, and at the same punishing him by means of abject humiliation*

Protection of Possessions

Being fully 'tooled up' might minimise one's chances of being attacked, but it is wise to contrive a few places about one's person in which to stash a wad of sterling in the event of being overpowered or beaten into surrender.

> Divide the money which you carry into several lots and sew some of the notes into the flaps of your waist-coat and others round the ankles. Another good place, except at sea or in a barber's shop, is inside the leather band of your hat. But a letter of credit is safer still.
>
> *The Happy Traveller*, Revd Frank Tatchell, 1923

Smugglers and drug runners are renowned for their habit of concealing contraband in the lower reaches of their digestive tracts. Whilst this is very effective in keeping valuables away from the depredations of muggers and thieves, it is a method that can hardly be recommended for use by a gentleman. Even so, provision should be made for the possibility of a brigand taking a larcenous shine to everything you possess.

> *Secret Jewels* – Before going to a rich but imperfectly civilised country, travellers sometimes buy jewels and bury them in their flesh. They make a gash, put the jewels in, and allow the flesh to grow over them as it would over a bullet. The operation is more sure to succeed if the jewels are put into a silver tube with rounded ends, for silver does not irritate. If the jewels are buried without a tube, they must have no sharp edges. The best place for burying them is in the left arm, at the spot chosen for vaccination. A traveller who has thus provided would always have a small capital to fall back upon, though robbed of everything he wore.
>
> *The Art of Travel*, Francis Galton, 1872

This technique is also useful for avoiding the petty bureaucracy of customs officials who may object to you importing items for augmenting your personal gemstone collection (Fig. 10).

Dangerous Animals

Fig. 10

When anticipating the threat of attack, do not overlook the dangers posed by vicious or deranged animals. Finding yourself at the business end of a slavering, bad tempered mutt can be almost as unpleasant as having to deal with a brigand, and it is likely be even less receptive to protestations and exhortations to reason.

The mongrel curs are a nuisance to the wayfarer in most foreign lands. It is useless to try and 'good dog' them. Instead, abuse them in the hoarsest voice at your command and with the worst language you can think of. They may slink off utterly ashamed of themselves, but, if one comes for you, try this method. Snatch off your hat and hold it out to him, when he will snap at it and seize it by the brim. Now the length of your hat and arm is exactly the length of your leg, and, if you kick out, he will get it just under the jaw, bite his tongue and go off howling. Approaching a dog sleeping in the road I do so whistling. This wakes him up before I get close and helps to convince him that I am human in spite of the bag on my shoulder and my outlandish smell.

The Happy Traveller, Revd Frank Tatchell, 1923

In all cases, face your foe with calmness and imperturbability.

The Rush of an Enraged Animal is far more easily avoided than is usually supposed. The way the Spanish bull-fighters play with the bull, is well known: any man can avoid a mere headlong charge . . . It is perfectly easy for a person who is cool to avoid an animal by dodging to one side or other of a bush. Few animals turn, if the rush be unsuccessful. The buffalo is an exception; he regularly hunts a man, and is therefore particularly dangerous. Unthinking persons talk of the fearful rapidity of a lion or tiger's spring. It is not rapid at all; it is a slow movement, as must be evident from the following consideration. No wild animal can leap ten yards, and they all make a high trajectory in their leaps. Now, think of the speed of a ball thrown, or rather pitched, with just sufficient force to be caught by a person ten yards off: it is a mere nothing.

The Art of Travel, Francis Galton, 1872

The spring of a lion or tiger may well be rather languid, but unfortunately what Mr Galton fails to point out is that such beasts do tend to run rather fast. No amount of prowess shown at the fathers' egg-and-spoon race at the school sports day can prepare you to outrun a cheetah, for example. To use the technique outlined above, the traveller should be prepared to stand his ground face-to-face with an animal, and keep his wits about him. After dodging a few initial charges, one soon gets the hang of it, and rather a pleasant afternoon can be spent side-stepping any manner of wildlife around a tent or a camp table whilst bolstering one's spirits by smoking cheroots and sipping champagne. (Fig. 11).

Fig. 11 *Big cats may look scary, with their large slavering mouths and sharp claws, but in actual fact they are slow-witted beasts that pose very little threat to a nimble fellow well tutored in the Military Two-Step*

CHAPTER THE THIRTEENTH

Suggesting Methods of Dealing with

EXTREMES OF
CLIMATE

EXTREMES OF CLIMATE

In the preceding chapters we have attempted to keep our advice as general as possible in relation to the weather conditions and geography that the traveller is likely to encounter, but it is now time for some more specific guidance on extremes of climate. As the thermometer and barometer soar or plummet to unpleasant and unnatural extents an adventurer will need to modify his clothing, expectations and attitudes in an attempt to remain comfortable, healthy and sane.

The Avoidance of Sun

Every year millions of British holidaymakers travel abroad with one object in mind: 'to catch a little sun'. Sunbathing is rumoured to be a very diverting and pleasurable pastime, but only for the locals, who will sit coolly on their verandas hooting with derision at the shambling procession of sun-worshippers as they file past on the way to the beach. For the sane traveller to tropical climes, however, keeping *out* of the sun should be his main priority.

Classically, in its natural state, an Englishman's flesh tends to be of a pleasing tone somewhere between off-white and duck-egg blue, and great pains should be taken to keep it that way. Even a modest exposure to the harmful rays of the sun will tend to damage the complexion, turning it a frightful pink, or even beige. The British Ambassador and his wife are hardly likely to take you seriously if you turn up at their cocktail party giving every appearance of having been lightly sautéed in unclarified butter.

Naturally, the best plan is to get your men to dig a large hole around 10ft deep and 6ft in diameter, in which to sit during the daylight hours. The top should be covered with an assortment of palm leaves and tarpaulins, and regular buckets of pina colada hoisted down in order to keep you cool and refreshed (Fig. 1). Alternatively a plan along traditional Indian lines may be employed.

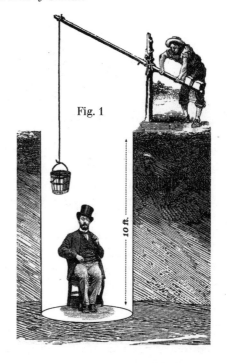

Fig. 1

When the sun is near the meridian for several hours a day on the plains of India, the native retires instinctively to the innermost apartment of his humble shed, where both light and heat are excluded. There he sits quietly in the midst of his family, regaling himself with cold water or sherbet, while a gentle perspiration flows from the skin, and contributes naturally and powerfully to his refrigeration. Mr Twining justly observes that the natives seem to suffer much from the hot season in Bengal. During the latter part of this season those natives whose circumstances enable them to act as they wish, avoid their food, and eat certain fruits which they consider cooling.

The Influence of Tropical Climates on European Constitutions,
James Ranald Martin, 1855

Packing for Hot Weather

Of course, if you have business to attend to then neither of the above solutions may be very practicable, and you will have to opt for wearing a costume specifically designed to ward off the worst effects of the sun. The following list should give you some idea of what you may wish to pack for a long weekend.

- *1 Light flannel coat, made to hook up, and with pockets to button, so that when you take off your coat and give it to some one to carry, the contents are not in danger of falling out.*
- *1 Pair light flannel trousers [Fig. 2]*
- *1 Pair light flannel knickerbockers*
- *2 Flannel shirts with breast pockets*
- *3 Merino singlets*
- *3 Pairs of merino or woollen socks*
- *3 Pairs of stockings*
- *2 Pairs of flannel pyjamas and jackets*
- *2 Japanese loose cotton gowns (yukata)*
- *1 Band or sash (san-yaku)*
- *Pocket handkerchiefs*
- *A plaid shawl or rug, required when sleeping on mountains.*
- *A pair of slippers*
- *1 Pair of stout walking boots*
- *1 Pair of white canvas shoes*
- *1 Sun hat and 2 white covers*
- *1 Cap*
- *1 Strong umbrella and 2 white covers.*

Fig. 2

Murray's Handbook for Travellers in Japan, 1884

* * *

The importance of flannel next the skin is so well-known that every traveller should adopt it, and it will be found beneficial equally in hot or cold climates. Next in excellence to flannel comes cotton, according to the common voice of all who know the tropics; linen is very improper, it strikes cold upon the skin.

Hardships in Travel Made Easy, 1864

The most important consideration for any traveller in the Tropics is proper protection of the head from the searing rays of the sun. Neglecting to make adequate provision in this department can have an unfortunate tendency to turn your cranium into a cooking vessel, and it is unlikely that you will be able to think clearly or come to any snappy business decisions if your thoughts are simultaneously being lightly poached in a cerebrospinal soup. Francis Galton suggests a 'wide-awake' hat (Fig. 3) for this purpose and adds that 'a muslin turban twisted into a rope and rolled round the hat is a common plan to keep the sun from the head and *spine*'. But this is only one ploy out of many for keeping the head at an acceptable regulo.

> An umbrella is a protection from the rain and from the sun; it should be of double silk or cotton, white without, green inside; but it is well to learn to dispense with so cumbersome an article. The best substitute is a cloth cap with a large vizor, with a thickly wadded white cover, and havelock hanging over the shoulders. The native saddlers make a convenient umbrella-case to affix to the saddle. Spectacles are useful as a protection from the glare of the sun. They should never be blue or neutral tint but green. A green veil is so offensive to the Turks as not unfrequently to subject the wearer to insult.
>
> *Murray's Handbook for Travellers in Constantinople*, 1871

* * *

In tropical countries the head and spine should be effectively protected, the level rays of the sun at morn or eve are often more dangerous than the vertical. The well-fitting ventilated pith-helmet, which forms

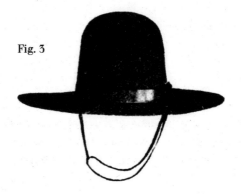

Fig. 3

Fig. 4a Fig. 4b

such a protective guard against the mid-day sun, does not equally
protect the sides of the head and the back of the neck from its hori-
zontal rays at morn and eve, at such times, therefore, a light curtain
of sufficient length should be attached to the rim of the helmet.

Hints to Travellers, 1883

The eminently sound advice given above has been further developed by Colonel Henry Macleod of the 2nd Poona Light Cavalry.
Having some off-cuts of ordinary domestic net curtain left over
after his bungalow was refurbished, he alighted upon the idea of
attaching these to the rim of his helmet using conventional steel
tracker rail. This enabled him to vary the amount of cover
afforded by the helmet, using the more conventional configura-
tion Fig. 4a for business or other situations where eye to eye
contact would seem desirable, and the arrangement in Fig. 4b
when he was feeling slightly more introspective and the area was
mercifully free from overly touchy Turks.

Health Issues in a Warm Climate

The mention of hot climates often conjures up images of sand
dunes and dry scorching winds, but more often than not the most
unbearable aspects of heat are experienced from humidity. For
an Englishman the sopping and oppressive conditions of the

rainforest or of the monsoon season on the Subcontinent represent the most uncivilised of all weather conditions. Humidity saps
him of his last ounce of volition, and can consequently bring the
building of bridges and the conquering of nations to a juddering
halt until more suitable weather arrives. Anyone who has experienced the advent of the rains in Hindustan will understand
completely:

> From the 15th of July to the 15th of October, and as the rain advances,
> we live in an atmosphere having all the properties of a tainted vapour-
> bath; and, when the winds come sifting through the Sunderbunds at
> the south-east, we experience many of the inconveniences ascribed by
> Hennen to the sirocco of the Mediterranean, which, 'without affecting
> the thermometer or barometer in any remarkable degree', yet inflicts
> on the delicately sensitive human frame a feeling of indescribable
> languor and oppression, with an exhausting perspiration, much like
> that we suffer from in Bengal during the latter part of the rainy season,
> and which a West Indian lady, speaking of the sirocco, described as
> giving 'the feel as if she had been bathing in a boiler of syrup.
>
> *Murray's Handbook for Travellers in India*, 1859

Apart from thwarting a man's ambitions, the oppressive heat of
the Tropics may affect a fellow badly in other ways too. Absent-
mindedly parading about in the sun all day, sans pith helmet and
tinted goggles, will inevitably lead to a bad bout of sunstroke, but
as we have seen this is a condition that can be readily treated by
bed rest and the trickling of salt water into the ears in the manner
described in Chapter 10. Further temperature-related maladies
include gogo, pinto, dobie itch, craw-craw, prickly heat and
gusset rot, but a far more insidious influence of the sun is its detrimental effects on the passions. The filthy heat of the Tropics, it
seems, can result in a corresponding surge in one's quota of filthy
thoughts too:

> *The Conduct and Government of the Passions* – Most of the precepts
> that apply to the regulation of the passions in cold climates, will be

found to apply to them in tropical climates; but it is necessary to correct at once an erroneous impression that there is something peculiar to the tropics which excite certain passions in a higher degree than in temperate regions. Dr Moseley says that, 'there is, in the inhabitants of hot climates, unless present sickness has an absolute control over the body, a promptitude and bias to pleasure, and an alienation from serious thought and deep reflection. The brilliancy of the skies, and the beauty of the atmosphere, conspire to influence the nerves against philosophy and her frigid tenets, and forbid their practice among the children of the sun.' However true this description may be in respect of 'the children of the sun', it does not accurately exhibit the condition of the strange European, in whom such a course of relaxation would be very immoral; for such a view would furnish the dissolute libertine with a *physical* excuse for his debaucheries, when the real source may be traced to the relaxation of religious and moral principals. We would ask Dr Moseley, if the '*promptitude* and bias to pleasure' be increased in a hot climate, the ability to pursue or practice it should be lessened? a fact well known to every debauchee.

The removal of religious and moral restraint, the temptation to vice, the facility of the means, and the force of example, are the real causes of this bias to pleasure, and in respect to the *effects* of licentious indulgences between the tropics, the reader may be assured that he will find, perhaps when too late, how much more dangerous and destructive they are than in Europe.

The nature of this supposed 'propensity' has been explained to him; and as the principal cause resides neither in the air, nor in the 'brilliancy of the skies', but in his own breast, he has no excuse for permitting it to grow into the wild luxuriance of unbridled excess.

The Influence of Tropical Climates on European Constitutions,
James Ranald Martin, 1855

I am constantly attempting to curb the wild luxuriance of unbridled excess in Mrs Darkwood too. This usually takes the form of an insatiable urge for shoes, handbags and soft furnishings, but it has been known to manifest itself in other ways too. In an attempt to curtail her *heat manias* I usually exhort her to take a cold bath in the hope that it will dampen her ardour a little. Sadly, my wife is never very responsive to cool reasoning and on one or two occasions I have had to take matters into my own hands, applying medication myself in the form of a pail of iced water.

Survival in a Cold Climate

Eking out an existence in the sweltering soup tureen of the Tropics is undoubtedly injurious to both health and morals, but questing into the icy wildernesses of the polar regions or climbing the snowy peaks of mountain ranges exposes the traveller to an entirely new level of danger. Even if he prepares his journey with the utmost care and professionalism, the explorer of chilly lands is bound to find himself in a constant battle for survival. Despite long months of preparation, at any moment he may find himself under threat from blizzards, avalanches, falls down crevasses or attacks from polar bears, not to mention frostbite, hypothermia, snow blindness and chilblains. Quite naturally the first priority is to come up with a few ruses for preventing oneself 'doing a Mallory' and perishing from exposure (Fig. 5). A fetching array of Fair Isle sweaters, a thick tweed hunting suit and large fur hat of Russian design can be added to as follows:

Whymper's tent; flannel shirts; under-waistcoats and drawers; long lamb's-wool stockings; woollen suit; fur coat, gloves

Fig. 5 *In sub-zero conditions items of clothing that one would not normally be seen dead in suddenly take on a new appeal*

and knitted sleeping-cap covering ears; flannel or blanket belt; woollen jersey comforters; Swiss woollen lined slippers, snow shoes; moccasins; hair eye-screens; wool, or fur rugs; warm gloves and mittens; patent Norwegian cooking apparatus; sleeping bags of woollen material or sheepskin, essential in high mountain excursions; canteens, fitted with enamel ironware; waterproof bags; tan canvas kit.

Hints to Travellers, Douglas W. Freshfield and
Captain W.J. Wharton, 1889

The fur coat is a particular necessity. Sable with ocelot trim (with angora lining) is always very stylish, and also serves as a useful badge of authority for an expeditionary leader, whereas Arctic fox or Polar bear are better suited to those who wish to be unassuming and blend in with their surroundings. Whichever style you opt for, the employ- ment of an Inuit valet is a tremendous boon in looking after fur garments properly.

Fig. 6 *Ladies planning to join an Antarctic expedition will need to modify their customary crinolines and silks in favour of a selection of furs*

Furs, if not too heavy – as they may easily be even in the coldest climates – are lighter and pleasanter than woollens, but are less durable and require care such as few white men know how to give. If not dried at frequent intervals, they rot and fall to pieces. If one expects to travel in the company of Indians or Eskimos who would take care of fur garments, these would prove the lightest and most comfortable apparel possible.

Handbook of Travel, Harvard Travellers' Club, 1917

Cold-proof Accommodation

Whether you are staying in a Whymper's tent or opting for a more permanent shelter, it is imperative that the temperature of the interior should be raised to an acceptable degree as rapidly as possible. Accumulating five burly explorers and six huskies in one small tent is one way of increasing the ambient temperature, but the effect can be added to if your comrades also have a mutual fondness for tobacco products.

> On one experimental trip Captain Parry was compelled by a sudden decrease of temperature to shelter his party in a small tent. They attempted to warm themselves by smoking, and found the temperature at their feet to be 1° below zero, while overhead the smoke had raised it to +7°, the outer air being –5°, soon falling –15°.
>
> *Shifts and Expedients of Camp Life*, Lord and Baines, 1876

Once heat is generated, it can be conserved by lagging your quarters with insulating materials. Modern products such as polystyrene foams and other non-conductors are all very well and good, but in these times of global warming a more organic, natural approach should be employed where possible.

> Should you at any time be so situated as to be compelled to winter on board ship in the Arctic regions, it will be well to follow the plan pursued by Dr Kane to render his ship and cabin as cold proof as possible. He procured large quantities of moss and turf, with which the quarter-deck was thickly covered. Down below he enclosed a space about 18 ft square, and packed the walls forming it, from floor to ceiling, with the same materials. The floor was carefully caulked with plaster of Paris and common paste, on this was laid a stratum of Manilla oakum 2in. thick, and over this deposit a canvas carpet was spread. The entrance was from the hold, by a long moss-lined passage or tunnel, formed after the manner in which the Esquimaux arrange the 'topsut,' or rabbit-burrow like passage which leads to their huts.
>
> *Shifts and Expedients of Camp Life*, Lord and Baines, 1876

Unlike home or, indeed, the Tropics, where cleanliness should be regarded as an absolute necessity, in a cold climate an explorer should be prepared to brush all guilt aside and ignore Nanny Bridlington's exhortations to 'always wash behind your ears'. Opting for a more easy-going approach to hygiene may be slightly unsettling to the house-proud, but can pay dividends for those wishing to avoid dying of hypothermia.

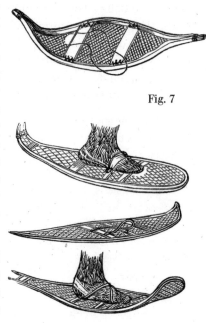

Fig. 7

The accumulation of seal and walrus flesh and blubber during the summer months makes these habitations disgustingly filthy; but it is to be remembered that the great necessity of the Esquimaux is to keep himself warm, and he cannot afford to lower the temperature of his skin by washing off the grease and dirt which encrust it.

Shifts and Expedients of Camp Life, Lord and Baines, 1876

Mobility in Polar Regions

A traveller will need to make special provision for getting about in polar regions. It might be assumed that the sturdy brogues that hold one in such good stead when tramping over grouse moors or trekking up the Cairngorms would also be perfect for polar exploration. On fine days this might be true, but with the onset of the first blizzard, and the snow rapidly accumulating to armpit level, it will become evident that you need more than stout footwear alone. An assortment of snow-shoes (Fig. 7) (for differing snow conditions) should be affixed to one's brogues to maintain mobility. For those in more of a hurry, a pair of skis or a dog sledge will be more suitable. Dogs are, indeed, the best animals for drawing a sledge, since ponies (as Captain Scott discovered to his cost) have an irritating tendency to die in sub-zero conditions. But do bear in mind that to manage a dog team successfully requires skill and discipline.

> The direction and speed of the team are regulated partly by the voice, but mainly by the whip . . . You must be able not only to hit any particular dog out of the team of twelve, but to accompany the feat also with a loud crack . . . The lash trails behind as you travel, and when thrown forward is allowed to extend itself, without an effort to bring it back. You wait patiently, after giving the projectile impulse until it unwinds its slow length, reaches the end of its tether, and cracks to tell you that it is at its journey's end. Such a crack on the ear or forefoot of an unfortunate dog is signalised by a howl quite unmistakable in its import.
>
> *Shifts and Expedients of Camp Life*, Lord and Baines, 1876

Fig. 8

Like humans, dogs can suffer terribly from chilblains and it is recommended that each dog be equipped with a quartet of husky brogues available from Dimmocks of Piccadilly, or those on a tight budget might opt for a home-made alternative (Fig. 8).

> During long journeys over rough and uneven ice the paws of dogs are liable to become worn and sore. It is well, therefore, before encountering such hindrances to travel, to protect them with moccasins.
>
> *Shifts and Expedients of Camp Life*, Lord and Baines, 1876

Scooting along at a bit of a lick will inevitably lead to a dramatic increase in the wind-chill factor and the traveller will need to make sure that his face is well protected from the sub-zero temperatures. Eskimo snow goggles together with a craftily constructed face-mask should ward off the worst evils of the climate.

Mask – Is merely a pocket-handkerchief, with strings to tie it over the face; eye-holes are cut in it, also a hole for the nose, over which a protecting triangular piece of linen is thrown, and another hole opposite the mouth, to breathe through; it is drawn below the chin so as to tie firmly in place. The mask prevents the face from being cut to pieces by the cold dry winds, and blistered by the powerful rays of the sun reverberated from the snow [Fig. 9].

The Art of Travel, Francis Galton, 1872

Overall, travelling in polar regions does not provide much by way of pleasure other than the satisfaction of knowing that you have done some sterling scientific research, that you have beaten some world record, or that you have managed to return with at least 80 per cent of your digits still intact. For those looking for something more than mere survival or world renown from a journey, the next chapter will provide some idea how one's time can be spent more entertainingly.

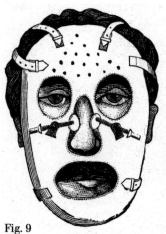

Fig. 9

CHAPTER THE FOURTEENTH

Recommending Various Popular

HOLIDAY PURSUITS

HOLIDAY PURSUITS

A large part of any journey overseas will, of course, be dedicated to manly and heroic tasks of an exploratory, scientific or commercial nature. After an arduous eighteen-month expedition it is frightfully important to return with several crates of notebooks containing trigonometric calculations of the heights of mountain ranges, mappings of obscure coastlines, sketches of ancient artefacts, and ambitious designs for proposed irrigation systems. These will be supplemented, no doubt, by a highly diverting, warts-and-all journal (detailing one's adventures living amongst the pygmies or the hairy Ainu) that will have the Royal Geographical Society (not to mention the tabloids) enthralled for months after.

Whilst setting up bauxite mines, teaching etiquette to the natives and discovering the sources of at least half a dozen rivers are an intrinsic part of an Englishman's travels, they should never be allowed to become all-consuming. Every now and then it is advisable to take some time off from the white man's burden and dedicate a few days purely to the pursuit of pleasure.

Big-game Hunting

For some unfathomable reason, there is a growing lobby today that maintains that killing things for fun should be outlawed as a legitimate leisure activity, but of all the pastimes loosely bundled under the heading of sport, surely none can be regarded as more stimulating than big-game hunting. Tracking things down and having a crack at them with your trusty Purdey is eminently good for health (yours rather than theirs), and also adds a bit of spice to the lives of animals that would otherwise spend most of their waking hours twiddling their claws pointlessly on the savannah wondering what on earth to do next. Whereas most other sports merely involve pitting one's wits against other men or the clock with not much at stake apart from a silver cup, self-esteem or a few front teeth, with big game one's life is constantly thrown into peril.

Fig. 1

As with most pursuits, the first consideration when hunting is how to dress appropriately. Unlike many other sports, big-game hunting involves a wardrobe mercifully free from spandex.

Complete Bush-costume – Mr Gordon Cumming describes his bush-costume as follows: 'My own personal appointments consisted of a wide-awake hat, secured under my chin by *rheimpys* or strips of dressed skin, a coarse linen shirt, sometimes a kilt, and sometimes a pair of buckskin knee-breeches, and a pair of *veldtschoens* or home-made shoes. I entirely discarded coat, waistcoat, and neck-cloth; and I always hunted with my arms bare; my heels were armed with a pair of powerful persuaders, and from my left wrist depended, by a double *rheimpy* (thong), an equally persuasive sea-cow *jambok* (whip of solid leather). Around my waist I wore two leather belts and girdles. The smaller did the duty of suspender, and from it on my left side depended a plaited *rheimpy*, eight inches in length, forming a loop, in which dangled my powerful loading-rod, formed of a solid piece of horn of the rhinoceros. The larger girdle was my shooting-belt; this was a broad leather belt, on which were fastened four separate compartments, made of otterskin, with flaps to button over, of the same material . . . Last, but not least, in my right hand I usually carried my double-barrelled two-grooved rifle, which was my favourite weapon.'

Fig. 2

The Art of Travel, Francis Galton, 1872

These days, when virtually everything we buy is made out of polyurethane, admixed with a sprinkling of microchips, semiconductors and Lycra, it is very refreshing that most of Mr Cumming's impedimenta is fashioned from natural products, including at least three endangered species. Such an enlightened eschewing of hydrocarbons should be heartily praised, and what could be kinder to the environment?

Deciding on the variety of animal you would like to bag is the next consideration. Each species will involve a different set of challenges:

Elephant – Except in vital spots the elephant absorbs 2-ounce balls as unconcernedly as a pin-cushion absorbs pins and in frontal attack his massive forehead is ample protection for the deep-seated brain against all but the strongest-hitting rifles. He has a good nose and ears but his eyes are poor, else elephant hunting would be suicide. Often he will overlook you in plain sight within a few feet if you do not move. The elephant kills with trunk, tusks and feet [Fig. 2].

Rhinoceros – If unable to stop a charge, sidestep when the rhinoceros is within a few paces. He will pass by straight as a railroad train, when you will have him at your mercy.

Cougar – The cougar is the least ferocious of the big cats and can only be considered dangerous if one tries to pet him.

Handbook of Travel, The Harvard Travellers' Club, 1917

Eventually a hunter can become so blasé about his skills as a
marksman that he might be tempted to make things more difficult for himself purely for the sport of it. Many a time an experienced sportsman has made a wager with his shooting
companions that he can bring down a rogue elephant or two with
one arm tied behind his back, or wandered off into lion-infested
scrubland wearing a blindfold and no trousers. Indeed, extreme
hubris can even lead to forgoing the effete luxury of firearms
altogether.

> The sportsman is generally provided with two guns, and with a spear
> as a *dernier ressort*, and most of the accidents which have happened
> have arisen either from foolhardiness or want of nerve . . . An
> Englishman, who for many years was a mighty bear hunter in Russia,
> was in the habit of attacking and pursuing these animals armed only
> with a spear, and although many were the deadly struggles that he
> had face to face with his grim opponent, he never met with any

Fig. 3 *Your travel tales simply won't be worth telling unless you have at least
one account of hand-to-hand combat with an enraged animal*

accident. To use the spear with any certainty requires great dexterity and strength of arm, with nerves of iron, and should on no account be attempted by a novice.

Murray's Handbook for Travellers in Russia, 1875

Whilst the above cannot be recommended for all, such excessive devil-may-caredom will have the advantage of making you very popular on the after-dinner speaking circuit. But be careful not to let a love of novel methods of slaughtering your prey descend into a wholesale emulation of the eccentric ways of the indigenous popoulation. Trying the technique outlined below, for example, will merely expose the hunter to the imminent danger of making a total ass of himself.

The Bushmen of Africa lie carefully concealed, with their bows and arrows, at a convenient distance from the nests of the birds or the edge of a vley or pool to which they come to drink. Stalking is an art the bushman excels in; and, with a piece of ostrich skin on his back, a stick roughly hewn into the form of the neck and head of the bird, together with his short bow, in the left hand, and a supply of arrows in his head band [Fig. 4] the cunning hunter creeps up wind towards the feeding flock.

Fig. 4

Shifts and Expedients of Camp Life, Lord and Baines, 1871

All sportsmen know of the mystical bond that develops between a predator and his quarry. Contrary to the squawkings of animal rights activists, it is common knowledge that the only pleasure a hunter gains from his sport is the thrill of the chase, and that nearly all animals regard being pursued as the most ripping fun.

Sadly, though, not all huntsmen adhere to the same code of sportsmanship, and there are some (typically those on a tight schedule, with a weight problem, or lacking patience) who may be drawn towards timesaving practices, resulting in very unsportsmanlike behaviour indeed.

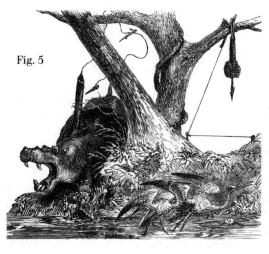

Fig. 5

Javelins – Heavy poisoned javelins, hung over elephant and hippopotamus paths, and dropped on a catch being touched, after the manner of a spring, are used generally in Africa. They sometimes consist of a sharp little assegai, or spike, most thoroughly poisoned, and stuck firmly into the end of a heavy block of thorn wood, about four feet long and five inches in diameter. This formidable affair is suspended over the centre of a sea-cow path, at about thirty feet from the ground, by a bark cord, which passes over a high branch of the tree, and thence, by a peg, on one side of a path beneath [Fig. 5].

The Art of Travel, Francis Galton, 1872

* * *

The steel traps manufactured at Oneida, on the Newhouse principle, are admirable, and range from the 'O' size, adapted for musk-rat, to No.7, or the 'great bear tamer' [Fig. 6].

Shifts and Expedients of Camp Life, Lord and Baines, 1871

Such methods cannot be dignified with the name of sport at all. Far from the sportsman being placed in mortal danger, he sets his trap and is then able to sit back in his tent puffing away on his pipe, sipping a brandy and reading the *Tatler*, waiting for an almighty hoo-hah to erupt from the undergrowth.

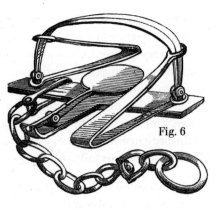

Fig. 6

Duelling

No holiday pursuit retains its appeal indefinitely, and gentlemen abroad may eventually become a bit jaded with taking pot shots at animals and elect, as a refreshing alternative, to start taking pot shots at each other instead.

Although duelling as a light-hearted pastime is chiefly suited to hot-headed youth, the odd occasion can arise in any man's life when he simply has to stand up for himself. Strictly speaking duelling is illegal in the United Kingdom, but abroad, whilst it is not exactly sanctioned by the law, a blind eye is usually turned to a man's need to defend his honour. As long as he is discreet, what he gets up to on a deserted beach or hilltop at 6 o'clock in the morning is very much his own business.

Generally things kick off over some perceived slur or other. For example, the rumour goes round that Mr A has been putting it about that Mr B is a bit of a stinker. Mr B, understandably, takes exception to this and demands satisfaction.

I myself have had to engage in a duel on only one occasion, not due to any allegations of stinkerhood but because some fellow was circulating scurrilous tittle-tattle regarding Mrs Darkwood and a supposed episode involving the entire rugby team of the Blues and Royals and a post-match bath. You can imagine my consternation some days after my ordeal (which I thankfully survived unscathed) when I discovered a rubber duck, a bottle of liniment and a musty sports sock behind one of the books in the library. To my great relief, Mrs Darkwood was quick to explain that one of her lady friends had given the artefacts to her as a jocular reference to the whole affair and they should be thought of, in a very real sense, as a trophy to my valour. How very touching, and just to think we sometimes accuse the ladies of lacking a sense of humour.

The process of instigating a duel commences with the challenge. This is offered by curtly slapping a fellow on both cheeks in the presence of witnesses, throwing a glove at his feet, and then sending him a carefully worded letter:

> The Italians are very laconic in their mode of wording these epistles; the following is a specimen:
>
> 'Sir, if your courage is equal to your impudence, you will meet me tonight in the wood.'
>
> Which sounds very warlike in the original, thus:
> *'Signore, s'il suo coraggio e grande come la sua impudenza m'incontra questa sera nel'Bosco.'*
>
> His cartel should be written carefully and expressed clearly, avoiding all strong language; simply stating, first, the cause of offence; secondly, the reason why he considers it his duty to notice the affair; thirdly, the name of his friend; and lastly, requesting a time and place may be appointed.
>
> *Art of Duelling*, by a Traveller, 1836

It is the named friend or Second who makes all the necessary arrangements – initially trying to defuse the situation but, failing this, hiring a surgeon and ensuring everyone is aware of the exact hour of the kick-off. This leaves the dueller to spend an uneasy night mentally preparing himself for the task in hand.

> That the mind may not dwell upon the affair, he ought to invite a few friends to dinner, and laugh away the evening over a bottle of port; or, if fond of cards play a rubber of whist. He should, however, carefully avoid drinking to excess, or taking any food that tends to create bile.
>
> *Art of Duelling*, by a Traveller, 1836

Friends should endeavour to reassure a nervous duellist that his chances of being killed are absolutely piffling compared to the odds on the three-legged nags that he invariably loses his shirt on at Chepstow.

Fig. 7

Persons generally imagine when they hear a man is about to fight a duel that he must be killed; and nine men out of ten, upon receiving a challenge, make their will, and get no sleep the night previous to their going out – that is, in this country. Abroad they treat the matter more lightly, as duels occur frequently, and they know from experience the risk of being killed is comparatively trifling . . . The chances of a man's being killed, are about fourteen to one; and of his being hit, about six to one.

Art of Duelling, by a Traveller, 1836

Come to think of it, in my experience, odds of six to one are usually given to a 'dead cert' in a horse-race, so it might be better to avoid any mention of odds and chances altogether, and merely give one's friend a few nuggets of advice on the niceties of duelling technique instead. To start with, standing a good twelve yards apart, the protagonists must learn to adopt the correct stance.

The attitude to be taken, is that which presents least surface [Fig. 7]; this being performed, it is always to be given over the right shoulder, which presents a surface more than one fourth less than a side face. I have known the ball make a groove across the ear, the side of the head grazed, and on two occasions, the side locks carried away; had the side face been presented, the consequences would have been fatal in all these cases.

The Young Man of Honour's Vade-Mecum, Abraham Bosquette, 1817

But even if a duellist suffers a hit (as long as it is not a *coup de coeur* or fatal shot) he should not let it worry him unduly. He should simply regard the matter as the source of many a future postprandial anecdote – that is, of course, once the bleeding has been staunched and wounds have healed.

Some of my acquaintances now living have received shots through the lungs and spleen. One, formerly an officer in the Hanoverian service, has been twice shot through the head; and, although, minus many of his teeth, and part of his jaw, he still survives, and enjoys good health [Fig. 8].

Art of Duelling, by a Traveller, 1836

In actual fact the dangers posed by one's opponent are relatively minor compared to potential 'collateral damage' resulting from 'equipment failure'.

Fig. 8a   Fig. 8b

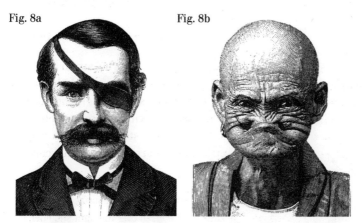

Fig. 8   *Exhibiting a selection of impressive duelling injuries can be very becoming in a man (a), but on no account let a passion for defending your honour disfigure you so much as to make you unacceptable in mixed company (b).*

It has been known, that by injudiciously over loading, the Principal has been killed by his own pistol bursting, a part of the barrel having entered the temple; and it has frequently happened, through the same cause, that the pistol-hand has been shattered to pieces. I was present on an occasion when the Principal shot his own Second through the cheek, knocking in one of his double teeth, not by the ball, but by part of the pistol barrel, that was blown out near the muzzle. I was also on the ground when a Principal shot himself through his foot, at the instep, which nearly cost him his life.

The Young Man of Honour's Vade-Mecum, Abraham Bosquette, 1817

It might be wise to prepare yourself for other eventualities too. The last thing you want is to turn up to the *releager* or meeting-place with a finely balanced brace of duelling pistols only to find that your opponent has decided that real satisfaction will only be served by attempting to slice you up into tiny little bits with his favourite sabre. As challengee you will have to accede to his request and you are bound to look a bit of a chump if you do not know one end of a sword from the other. Therefore, make sure your skills span various disciplines, and remember: practice makes perfect.

Fig. 9

Duelling with a Sword – To accustom a man to the appearance of a naked blade when opposed to him, I constructed an apparatus made in the following manner:- I procured a strong iron spring, wormed in a conical shape, with the base riveted into a small iron plate pierced with four holes: this I screwed into the wall of my chamber. At the smallest end of the spring was fixed a socket, into which the blade of a fencing sword fitted.

Frequently for an hour at a time I have stood before it with my foil, thrusting, parrying, and keeping it constantly in motion. In this way the nervous feeling produced by the point of a naked weapon may be in some measure overcome – as much, at least, as is possible by artificial means. The wrist also acquiring a degree of strength and pliability, that enables a man to handle his sword more expertly [Fig. 9].

Art of Duelling, by a Traveller, 1836

Intriguingly disfigured with bullet holes and duelling scars, the traveller will be guaranteed the respect of fellow men and the devotion of the ladies but, thoroughly enervated by conflict, the wanderer may wish to retire to the beach and indulge in a slightly more conventional and relaxing pastime.

Swimming

A gentleman's holiday pursuits need not be wholly devoted to competition or bloodlust in order to be enjoyable. Naturally, to relax an Englishman habitually repairs to an art gallery, theatre or tavern, but it is possible to unwind in more health-giving ways too. Bobbing about in the surf can be quite exhilarating, but does require a modicum of skill to avoid immediate drowning. Buoyancy is achieved by moving the arms and legs in a co-ordinated manner (Figs. 10 and 11). It is well to learn the basic technique prior to departure.

Learning to Swim – A good way of teaching a person to swim, is a modification of that adopted at Eton. The teacher may sit in a punt or on a rock, with a stout stick of 6 or 10 feet in length, at the end of which is a cord of 4 feet or so, with loops. The learner puts himself into the loops; and the teacher plays him, as a fisherman would play a fish, in water that is well out of his depth: he gives him just enough support to keep him from drowning.

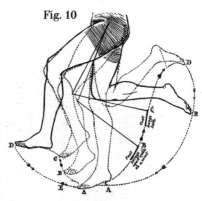

Fig. 10

The Art of Travel, Francis Galton. 1872

Once the rudiments have been mastered, you will have *carte blanche* to fling yourself into every pond, river or sizeable puddle from East Purley to Kathmandu. But there are certain circumstances under which bathing is not strictly wise.

When to Bathe – Delicate persons should never bathe before breakfast; between 10 a.m. and noon is the best time of the day for such people to swim. Those who do go for a 'dip before breakfast' should eat a biscuit before entering the water. This, bear in mind, is no permission to eat a hearty meal, which is a most harmful practice just prior to a swim at any time of the day. Do not go into the water when you feel cold, when you feel hot, when you have a headache, or when it is raining. If the place selected for your initial attempt is near houses, look to see if any broken glass or crockery is lying about. Such fragments inflict nasty wounds if trodden upon.

Swimming, Montague A. Holbein, 1903

Whilst swimming abroad, the traveller should also be constantly on the lookout for crocodiles, sharks, speeding motorboats, rogue currents, Portuguese men-o'-war, tsunamis, piranhas, and canoes full of natives brandishing spears. In a blind panic to get away from these menaces a swimmer is liable to inhale more water than would seem generally conducive to

Fig. 11

consciousness. If you are able to make it to shore, ensure you do not lack a couple of burly but gentle comrades to help you regain your composure.

> *Drowning* – A half-drowned man must be put in bed in dry, heated clothes, hot stones, &c., placed against his feet, and his head must be raised moderately. Human warmth is excellent, such as that of two big men made to lie close up against him, one on each side. All rough treatment is not only ridiculous but full of harm; such as the fashion – which still exists in some places – of hanging up the body by the feet, that the swallowed water may drain out of the mouth.
>
> *The Art of Travel*, Francis Galton, 1872

So maybe swimming is not quite as relaxing as it first seems. The best advice is to restrict one's aquatic adventures to the fully-heated swimming pools of one's wealthy American friends. A tight bathing cap will ward off ear-ache, a large inflatable life belt and pair of water wings will minimise the chances of drowning, and a capacious flute of Bollinger should dispel any desire to exert oneself.

Pig-Sticking

The tranquil life of the fishes can only satisfy a man for so long, and inevitably before one's journey comes to an end the pull of the sports field will beckon once more. Other than the immense draw of big game, there are some smaller prey that can be just as challenging. Pig-sticking is to big-game hunting what a cheeky Beaujolais Nouveau is to a majestic Grand Cru. A combination of polo, jousting and fox-hunting, pig-sticking is the ideal pastime for a young man with bags of energy and very few scruples about skewering a wild boar to death with multiple stab wounds whilst travelling at 35 miles per hour. Equipped with a bamboo spear (eight to ten feet long) (Fig. 12), a nimble steed and an abnormally high level of testosterone, up to three 'spears' meet early in the day and prepare for action.

> There is the start in the early morning with, at the most, three spears in all. A small line of five elephants, with led horses filling up the gaps. Grass and jhow jungle as far as the eye can see, broken up by small streams, many of them with steep sides covered with jungle, and heavy muddy bottoms, clumps of thick wood dotted about, and the hills of Nepal as a background to all. Nothing is to be heard but the swish of the elephants trumping through the grass, when in a second this peaceful scene is changed to one of wild excitement by the time-honoured cry of 'Wuh Jata' ('There he goes'), and right enough, an old boar is viewed stealing away on the right. The three spears are off in hot pursuit.
>
> Major F.W. Mackenzie quoted in *Modern Pig-Sticking*,
> A.E. Wardrop, 1914.

Those fortunate enough to have taken part in a spot of pig-sticking will be aware that it is all too easy to get carried away with the excitement of it all. But at least there will be something to recall and wax effusive about in the autumn of one's life.

> The wild boar! There is something in the very name suggestive of fierce, impetuous courage, of dogged, obstinate determination, and

Fig. 12 *Galloping in pursuit of a pig is an energetic sport, but in reality merely requires the same level of skill as the average billiards player hitting a tricky drop-shot, only on horseback and at 35 miles per hour*

sudden, brisk rapidity of action . . . What a tumultuous crowd and whirl of feelings memory recalls as it dwells on the associations connected with the pursuit of that animal! How vividly it reflects all the accessories of that noble sport, termed, indifferently, 'Hog-hunting,' or, less euphoniously, 'Pig-sticking!' The preparations for, and happy prospect of, the meet! the excitement and expectation attending the period before the break! the wild feeling of enjoyment, the sense of relief, of being, as it were, unstrapped, as the 'gone away' is seen or announced! Then the run! the interest with which the relaxing speed of the panting game is viewed! the intensity of the eagerness to draw forward! the spirited emulation! the racy contest for the honour of *first-spear*! the game Arab horse reeling from exhaustion and hard pressing, but struggling for victory as keen as his master, every stride a struggle! the last desperate effort! the lift with hand and heel! the lunge of the body forward over the gallant horse's neck! the thrust at arm's length, almost involving separation from the saddle! a gentle touch – yes – no – by heavens, yes! – the *first spear* is won. Hurrah! hurrah!

Hog-Hunting in the East, Captain. J.T. Newall, 1867

Fig. 13

I am very much afraid that Nanny Bridlington would not look with favour on the use of punctuation in this paragraph. She would have cheerfully broken one or two of my little childhood fingers if I had attempted to write such prose. It can only be concluded that Captain Newall's excessive use of the exclamation mark as displayed above is the result of a breathless excitability exacerbated by an over-indulgence in port.

CONCLUSION

A curious thing tends to happen around eighteen months into an expedition. The endless routine of living under canvas; slaughtering and collecting vast quantities of the local fauna; constructing roads, mines, oil refineries and railways; acquiring lorry-loads of artworks and antiquities; introducing foreigners to the Englishman's genteel concepts of fair play, queuing and afternoon tea – all these will suddenly lose their shine and begin to pall. At this point the adventurer must decide if this is nature's way of telling him that his travels are at an end, or whether it is worth forging on, despite his misgivings, in pursuit of the next goal, such as the lost temple of Phu Kham Chan or some equally enticing prospect. Increasingly the contents of Nanny Bridlington's pantry will start to loom large once more over his nocturnal imaginings, and the decision whether to stay or return to Blighty will fill each day with a creeping restlessness.

> When your journey draws near its close, resist restless feelings; make every effort before it is too late to supplement deficiencies in your various collections; take stock of what you have gathered together, and think how the things will serve in England to illustrate your journey or your book.
>
> *The Art of Travel*, Francis Galton, 1872

If a return to civilisation is the decision, a homecoming at the end of a very long journey, as with the completion of any lengthy and demanding enterprise, may seem rather anticlimactic. Despite the rapturous welcome of friends at

the club, the gratitude of the Ashmolean and British Museums, not to mention the admiring glances from the young ladies in the typing pool of the Royal Geographical Society, the traveller may well feel somewhat deflated. He will probably be prone to a good deal of self-examination, asking himself some very serious questions such as: 'What on earth has it all meant? What has it all been for? Will my wife still love me with a face disfigured by disease? How will I ever rid myself of these blasted tapeworms?' But this is a very natural phase in any journey and in time will pass.

In exchange for all his hardships and suffering the returned wanderer may expect to gain some very precious benefits.

Sympathy and tolerance, acquisitions of great price, are the reward of your journeying. Having mixed much with your fellow men, you view mankind from a new angle and have gained the charitable outlook that only comes with seeing the world. And, as you grow older, you will be ever better company for yourself, having remembered, what so many of us forget, that, to have pleasant memories then, we must contrive for them now. At any rate, there is small risk of your becoming that miserable thing, a disappointed man, nor will it ever be said of you, as it was of one who had wasted his life: 'His days

should have been a rosary of priceless pearls, and he let them slip
through his fingers like beads of common glass.'

The Happy Traveller, Revd Frank Tatchell, 1923

With the indignities of travel fresh in his mind the adventurer will
probably swear never to embark on a lengthy journey ever
again – and at the time may even really mean it. Having convinced oneself that the last expedition has secured enough
amusing anecdotes to sew up the after-dinner speaking circuit for
several years to come, and an impressive portfolio of overseas
business concerns into the bargain – one might imagine that
staying put was by far the best option. But the road of domestic-
ity can often be as rocky and badly cambered as a yak trail in the
Khangai mountains – hugely unpleasant to journey along and
liable to produce serious bruising. Before long, fresh plans will
start to unfold. The prospect of gathering more 'priceless pearls'
to ruminate over in your dotage will cause the cycle of departure
and return to recommence.

When one finally does reach decrepitude, and hangs up the
crampons, sou'wester, cleft sticks and leech gaiters for one last
time, at least it will be with the certainty that the insufferable
humidity and disease and the incessant jabbering of abroad are
well behind one and one's future will be green and pleasant
forever more.

If we suppose the judicious traveller to be an Englishman; when after having visited Europe, he reflects on the different climates, productions, and governments, peculiar to the various nations; that some are parched by droughts which continue half of the year; that others appear as if situated under a dripping sponge; others buried under snow; subject to earthquakes; exposed to the ravages of volcanoes, or to irresistible inundations; and others overrun by wild beasts and venomous animals; he will then be sensible, that in England he may spend a greater number of days in the open air, than in any other country. And when he considers the arbitrary and tyrannic governments, the slavery and poverty of the lower class of people, the pride and ignorance of the opulent, and the superstition and bigotry of both, and compares them to the advantages which so eminently distinguish his own country, where the climate is temperate, the earth fruitful, the government mild, the inhabitants (of both sexes) intelligent, and the women remarkably beautiful – he will then rest contented with the happiness he enjoys, by having it in his power to spend the remainder of his days in 'Happy England'.

Richard Twiss quoted in *The Traveller's Oracle*, Dr William Kitchiner, 1827

BIBLIOGRAPHY

Army and Navy Co-operative Society, *Yesterday's shopping: the Army & Navy Stores catalogue, 1907* (David & Charles, 1969)

The Art of Duelling, by a Traveller (Joseph Thomas, 1836)

Baedeker, Karl, *The Traveller's Manual of Conversation in Four Languages, English, French, German, Italian* (London, 1886)

Bellairs, Nona Maria Stevenson, *Going Abroad, or, Glimpses of art and character in France and Italy* (C.J. Skeet, 1857)

Bosquette, Abraham, *The Young Man of Honour's Vade-Mecum* (C. Chapple, 1817)

Buchan, William M.D., *Buchan's Domestic medicine* (T. Cadell & W. Davies, 1803)

Cook, Thomas, and Son, *Cook's Tourist's Handbook for Northern Italy* (Hodder & Stoughton, 1875)

Coxwell, Henry Trace, *My Life and Balloon Experiences* (W.H. Allen & Co., 1887)

Croal, Thomas A., *A Book About Travelling, Past and Present* (William P. Nimmo, 1877)

Cringle, Tom, *Tom Cringle's Log* (William Blackwood, 1833)

Dawson, Edwin Collas, *Lion-Hearted, The Story of Bishop Hannington's Life* (Seeley & Co., 1890)

Duncan, Martin, *The Transformations of Insects* (Cassell, Petter, Galpin & Co., 1882)

Eric, Writer on Hunting, *Ten Days 'Casual' with Ladies after Tiger* (India: 1916)

Erskine, F.J., *Tricycling for ladies or hints on the choice and management of tricycles with suggestions on dress, riding and touring* (Iliffe & Son, 1884)

Ferris, Richard, *How to Fly* (New York: Thomas Nelson & Sons, 1910)

Fonvielle, Wilfrid de, *Adventures in the Air* (Translated and Edited by John S. Keltie, 1877)

Ford, Richard, *A Handbook for Travellers in Spain* (John Murray, 1847)

Freshfield, Douglas W. and Wharton, Captain W.J.L., *Hints for Travellers* (Royal Geographical Society, 1889)

Galton, Sir Francis, *The Art of Travel* (John Murray, 1872)

Giles, Herbert Allen, *Chinese without a Teacher, Easy and Useful Sentences in the Mandarin Dialect* (Shanghai: 1872)

Gomme, George Laurence, *English Traditions and Foreign Customs* (Elliot Stock, 1885)

Gregory A. T., *A Practical Swiss Guide . . . By an Englishman in Switzerland* (London, 1856)

Handbook of Travel (Cambridge, USA: Harvard University Press, 1917)

A Handbook of Travel-Talk in English, German, French and Italian (London, 1856)

Hardships made easy. Domestic hardships. Hardships in travel. Hardships abroad (London, 1864)

Hawes, Sir Benjamin, *A narrative of an ascent to the summit of Mont Blanc, made during the summer of 1827 by Mr. W. Hawes* (London, 1828)

Hey, Richard, *A Dissertation on Duelling* (William Smith, 1801)

How to Drive a Motorcar, by the staff of *The Motor* (Temple Press, 1914)

Holbein, Montague A., *Swimming.* (C. Arthur Pearson, 1903) (Republished Bloomsbury/ Octopus 2005)

Holt, Emily, *Encyclopædia of Etiquette* (McClure, Phillips & Co., 1901)

Hull, Edmund C.P., *The European in India; or, Anglo Indian's Vade-Mecum* (R.S. Mair, 1878)

Johnson, James, *The influence of tropical climates, more especially the climate of India, on European constitutions; the principal effects and diseases thereby induced, their prevention or removal, and the means of preserving health in hot climates, rendered obvious to Europeans of every capacity* (printed for J. Callow, medical bookseller, London, 1815)

Kitchiner, William, *The Traveller's Oracle; or, Maxims for Locomotion* (Henry Colburn, 1827)

Kocheim, Amalia von, *A Handbook of foreign cookery, principally French, German and Danish* (London, 1845)

Longman's Practical Swiss Guide (1856)

Landor, Arnold Henry Savage, *Alone with the Hairy Ainu* (John Murray, 1893)

Leonard, Arthur Glyn, *The Camel: its uses and management* (Longman & Co., 1894)

Lord, William Barry, and Baines, Thomas, *Shifts and Expedients of Camp Life* (Horace Cox, 1876)

Lowndes, George R., *Gipsy Tents, and how to use them* (The Field Office, 1890)

Martin, James Ranald, Sir, *The influence of tropical climates on European constitutions: including practical observations on the nature and treatment of the diseases of Europeans on their return from tropical climates.* (J. Churchill, 1856)

Martineau, Harriet, *Eastern Life, present and past* (John Murray, 1848)

May, Gustav, *Ballooning: a concise sketch of its history and principles* (1885)

Mecredy, Richard James, *The Art and Pastime of Cycling* (Dublin: Mecredy & Kyle, 1890)

Mellis, Captain C.J., *Lion-Hunting in Somali-Land* (Chapman & Hall, 1895)

Murray's Handbook for Travellers in the Bengal Presidency (John Murray, 1882)

Murray's Handbook for Travellers in the Bombay Presidency (John Murray, 1881)

Murray's Handbook for Travellers in India; being an account of the three presidencies, and of the overland route (John Murray, 1859)

Murray's Handbook for Travellers in Central & Northern Japan (John Murray, 1884)

Murray's Handbook for Travellers on the Continent: being a guide through Holland, Belgium, Prussia, and Northern Germany, and along the Rhine, from Holland to Switzerland (John Murray, 1836)

Murray's Handbook for Travellers in Constantinople, the Bosphorus, Dardanelles, Brousa, and Plain of Troy (John Murray, 1871)

Murray's Handbook for Travellers in Denmark, Norway, Sweden, and Iceland (John Murray, 1858)

Murray's Handbook for Travellers in Lower and Upper Egypt (John Murray, 1896)

Murray's Handbook for Travellers in Greece (John Murray, 1884)

Murray's Handbook for Travellers in the Panjáb, Western Rajpútáná, Kashmír, and Upper Sindh (John Murray, 1883)

Murray's Handbook for Travellers in Portugal (John Murray, 1855)

Murray's Handbook for Travellers in Russia, Poland, and Finland; including the Crimea, Caucasus, Siberia, and Central Asia (John Murray, 1875)

Murray's Handbook for Travellers in Sicily: including Palermo, Messina, Catania, Syracuse, Etna, and the ruins of the Greek temples (John Murray, 1864)

Murray's Handbook for Travellers in Sweden (John Murray, 1883)

Newall, J.T., *Hog Hunting in the East, and other sports* (London, 1867)

Nugent, Thomas, *The Grand Tour* (London, 1749)

Powell, Baden Fletcher Smythe Baden-, *Ballooning as a sport* (Edinburgh & London: William Blackwood & Sons, 1907)

Royal Geographical Society, *Hints to Travellers* (1883)

Steel, John Henry, *A manual of the diseases of the elephant and of his management and uses* (Madras: W.H. Moore, 1885)

Sinclair, Archibald and Henry, William, *Swimming* (Longmans, Green, and Co., 1908)

Steere, Edward, *A Handbook of the Swahili Language* (London: 1918)

Tatchell, Revd Frank, (Vicar of Midhurst), *The Happy Traveller, A Book for Poor Men* (Methuen & Co., 1923)

The Tourists' Annual, A new guide by road, rail, and water to highways and byways at home and abroad, etc. (1868)

Twiss, Richard, *Travels Through Portugal and Spain* (G. Robinson, 1775)

Vyse, Griffin W., *An English-man in a Harem* (Simpkin, Marshall & Co., 1887)

Wardrop, A.E., *Modern pig-sticking* (Macmillan, 1914)

Wilkinson, John Gardner, Sir., *Modern Egypt and Thebes: being a description of Egypt, including the information required for travellers in that country* (London, 1843)

Winans, Walter, *Hints on Revolver Shooting* (New York & London: G.P. Putnam's Sons, 1904)

Wit and wisdom: How to live on £1 a week. (published at the office of *Wit and Wisdom* ca. 1890)

'Wyvern' (Arthur Robert Kenney Herbert), *Culinary Jottings for Madras* (Madras: Higginbotham and Co., 1883)

ACKNOWLEDGEMENTS

Mr Darkwood would like to thank:
Nanny Bridlington, Jane Challenger Gillitt,
Mrs Darkwood, Edward Faulkner,
Shaun Ferguson, Dr Reinhardt Flünkduster,
Maria Teresa Gavazzi, Kate Harvey,
Stephen Jolly of Mythop, Christophe Lienhard,
Ginnie Murray, John Murray, Colonel Pearce,
Susan Smith, Stourbridge,
Naomi Tummons and Peter Tummons,
for their assistance in the writing of this book.

Thanks to Bloomsbury Publishing/Octopus Publishing
for permission to print an extract from *Swimming*
by Montague A. Holbein